Fodor's

25 Best

HONG KONG

How to Use This Book

KEY TO SYMBOLS

🗺 Map reference to the accompanying fold-out map

✉ Address

☎ Telephone number

🕐 Opening/closing times

🍴 Restaurant or café

🚃 Nearest rail station

Ⓜ Nearest subway or MTR (Mass Transit Railway) station

🚌 Nearest bus route

⛴ Nearest riverboat or ferry stop

♿ Facilities for visitors with disabilities

❓ Other practical information

▷ Further information

ℹ Tourist information

✋ Admission charges: Expensive (more than HK$200) Moderate (HK$50–HK$200 Inexpensive (HK$50 or less)

This guide is divided into four sections

● Essential Hong Kong: An introduction to the city and tips on making the most of your stay.
● Hong Kong by Area: We've broken the city into four areas, and recommended the best sights, shops, entertainment venues, nightlife and restaurants in each one. Suggested walks help you to explore on foot.
● Where to Stay: The best hotels, whether you're looking for luxury, budget or something in between.
● Need to Know: The info you need to make your trip run smoothly, including getting about by public transport, weather tips, emergency phone numbers and useful websites.

Navigation In the Hong Kong by Area chapter, we've given each area its own color, which is also used on the locator maps throughout the book and the map on the inside front cover.

Maps The fold-out map with this book is a comprehensive street plan of central Hong Kong. The grid on this map is the same as the grid on the Hong Kong Island and Kowloon area locator maps and has upper case grid references. Sights and listings within the New Territories area have lower case grid references.

Contents

Introducing Hong Kong

Amid the low-key islands of the Asian tropics, Hong Kong stands tall in glass and steel. For over a century, this city of 7.3 million has extended a welcome to guests charmed by its beguiling mix of macho Western capitalism and Eastern mores.

From earliest colonial days, Hong Kong's wild islands, bays and mountains have been part of the appeal, but the city's lure veers toward the man-made. Designer shops, restaurants and trendy bars abound within the urban jungle. Looking down at it all after dark from Victoria Peak is nothing short of metropolis-shaped seduction.

The ride has been turbulent since 1997. At first there was economic uncertainty and population shifts. The Asian Financial Crisis hit just as the British sailed out, bird flu and SARS drove tourists away, and protests erupted over political interference from Beijing. Things have sometimes seemed shaky. Hong Kongers, however, are a special breed—resilient, hard working. They embrace Western ideas but traditional Chinese culture is strong. The Special Administrative Region of Hong Kong had a difficult first decade, but these difficulties have made it stronger. You'll see people in the parks practising t'ai chi, an ancient exercise routine, as often as you'll see a string of joggers.

In amongst the melee, Hong Kong rebranded itself as one of the most dynamic economies and cultures in the world. Newly moneyed China has forced Hong Kong to reassess its sense of superiority, but the booming mainland tourist trade has driven glitzy new developments in hotels, restaurants and infrastructure.

Modern Hong Kong society has money on its mind but it's combined with cultural savvy and a global outlook. Hong Kong has had its challenges in its two decades of independent rule, but it's survived them all to emerge more vibrant than ever.

FACTS AND FIGURES

- Population of Hong Kong: 7.3 million.
- 75 percent of Hong Kong's territory is rural or country park.
- Since the first reclamation project began in the 1850s, some 45sq miles (117sq km) of new land has been created.
- The Hong Kong–Zhuhai–Macao Bridge is the world's longest sea bridge, spanning 34 miles (55km).

WORKING TOGETHER

Hong Kong is slowly becoming more integrated with mainland China. Though mainland Chinese have been blamed for everything from inflating property prices to overburdening the health system, the mainland has been vital to the city's economic revival. There's a reason why young Hong Kongers can speak Mandarin, the mainland lingo.

BEGINNINGS

After being ceded to the British in 1842, Hong Kong Island thrived as a colonial trading hub. Jardine, Matheson and Co. dominated business, dealing in cotton, tea and opium. Clippers from India were spied from a peak above Causeway Bay, sometimes with chasing pirates. Indeed, the Noonday Gun, a surviving cannon, was one of the company's anti-piracy safeguards.

SOFT SKILLS

China's post-1980s opening up means Hong Kong is no longer the vital stepping stone for trade between East and West. However, it's remained king in the soft services of globalization—finance and insurance—and has worked hard to attract tourists from around the world. Despite the frenetic pace and heat, Hong Kongers are unfailingly polite, friendly and welcoming.

5

A Short Stay in Hong Kong

DAY 1

Morning After a buffet breakfast at your hotel, head straight for **The Peak** (▷ 38–39) taking the Peak Tram to view the city and the outlying islands stretched out before you. There are 360-degree views from the Sky Terrace 428 at the top of the Peak Tower for an entrance fee, but you can enjoy views for free atop The Peak Galleria mall.

Mid-morning Back in Central, head for **Cat Street Market** (▷ 44) where tiny shops teem with antiques and bric-a-brac.

Lunch Enjoy a good-value set lunch at one of the diners on Elgin Street.

Afternoon What better way to experience the real Hong Kong than to take a ride on the **Star Ferry** (▷ 60–61) to Kowloon, where you can take in the museums of the Tsim Sha Tsui Waterfront or indulge in a little retail therapy on Nathan or Canton roads.

Mid-afternoon For a break from shopping, try afternoon tea at the **InterContinental** lobby lounge (▷ 112) with its quiet luxury and spectacular views of the harbor.

Dinner Before dinner make sure you're at the clock tower at 8pm to watch the nightly **Symphony of Lights** (▷ 62–63), which illuminates the harbor. For dinner, if you can get a reservation, return to the island and try **Caprice** (▷ 48) where the superb French cuisine and art nouveau surroundings make for a lavish evening.

Evening Take the Mid-Levels Escalator (an experience in itself; ▷ 30) to SoHo for a few drinks in **Staunton's Wine Bar** (▷ 47). Then to Lan Kwai Fong for some fun in one of the many bars.

DAY 2

Morning Hop on the MTR Tung Chung line to **Lantau Island** (▷ 96–97, 98). Kick off the morning with a 30-minute cable-car ride on the Ngong Ping 360 gondola. Enjoy panoramic views before arriving at Ngong Ping Village, where you can wander around the outlets, take part in a tea ceremony, or experience the immersive Walking with Buddha exhibition.

Mid-morning Walk over to the **Tian Tan Buddha** (▷ 96–97), then climb up the 268 steps to admire the Buddha and the museum inside.

Lunch Enjoy a vegetarian lunch at the **monastery** (▷ 96), or if you are craving meat, ride the cable car back to Tung Chung to try what's on offer at the food outlets there.

Afternoon Head out to Kowloon and make your way to the **Ladies' Market** in Mong Kok (▷ 68), where you can try your hand at bargaining for inexpensive clothes. Stop by at the **Nelson Street Wetmarket**, where the produce is sold from buckets and tubs and filleted to order.

Mid-afternoon Don't forget to seek out the bird market in **Yuen Po Street** where you can watch the caged birds sing while their owners feed them crickets with chopsticks.

Dinner Head to **Mong Kok** (▷ 68) for an authentic Chinese dinner. Try Michelin-starred **Ming Court** (▷ 75) at Cordis Hotel , which comes highly recommended as one of the best Cantonese restaurants in the city.

Evening Knutsford Terrace has a more local atmosphere than SoHo or Lan Kwai Fong, and has bars to suit all tastes.

Top 25

These pages are a quick guide to the Top 25, which are described in more detail later. Here they are listed alphabetically and the tinted background shows the area they are in.

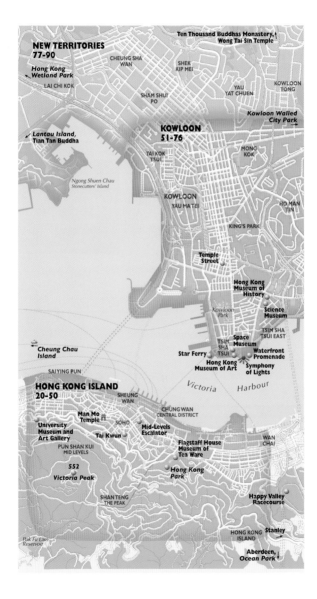

NEW TERRITORIES
77-90

Hong Kong Wetland Park

CHEUNG SHA WAN

SHEK KIP MEI

LAI CHI KOK

Ten Thousand Buddhas Monastery, Wong Tai Sin Temple

SHAM SHUI PO

YAU YAT CHUEN

KOWLOON TONG

Lantau Island, Tian Tan Buddha

KOWLOON
51-76

Kowloon Walled City Park

TAI KOK TSUI

MONG KOK

Ngong Shuen Chau Stonecutters' Island

KOWLOON
YAU MA TEI

HO MAN TIN

KING'S PARK

Temple Street

Hong Kong Museum of History

Science Museum

Kowloon Park

TSIM SHA TSUI EAST

Cheung Chau Island

Space Museum

Waterfront Promenade

SAI YING PUN

Star Ferry

TSIM SHA TSUI

Hong Kong Museum of Art

Symphony of Lights

HONG KONG ISLAND
20-50

SHEUNG WAN

Victoria Harbour

Man Mo Temple

SOHO

CHUNG WAN
CENTRAL DISTRICT

University Museum and Art Gallery

Tai Kwun

Mid-Levels Escalator

WAN CHAI

PUN SHAN KUI
MID LEVELS

Flagstaff House Museum of Tea Ware

552
Victoria Peak

Hong Kong Park

SHAN TENG
THE PEAK

Happy Valley Racecourse

Pok Fu Lam Reservoir

HONG KONG ISLAND

Stanley

Aberdeen, Ocean Park

ESSENTIAL HONG KONG TOP 25

Shopping

Hong Kong is a great place for shopping. For visitors there are the many craft items to take home as souvenirs, but another reason to shop in Hong Kong is that many items such as cameras, electronics, clothes, shoes and glasses can be cheaper here than in Europe. American visitors may snap up a few bargains, too, but it's best to research prices before kicking off a shopping spree. Also, on big-ticket items, you may be charged import duties on your return trip.

Emporia and Flea Markets

The most popular items among visitors can be found in the big Chinese emporia and flea markets. Look for hand-embroidered silk shawls and blouses, Chinese slippers, as well as gorgeous silk cushion covers and bedspreads. There are lots of tailors in Hong Kong who can make suits or shirts within a few days at relatively inexpensive prices. For bargain hunters there are many factory shops and outlets, where all kinds of seconds and end-of-run clothes are available at a fraction of the retail price. However, these places can be hit or miss, depending on the day. Another serious contender for your vacation funds is jewelry, either made with semiprecious stones, jade or cloisonné. Gold jewelry is beautifully made, often using Chinese characters as a design

BARGAINING

Bargaining is an essential part of the shopping experience in Hong Kong markets. Don't try it in department stores or other fixed-price establishments, but in the markets or smaller shops negotiation is expected and essential. Before bargaining you should know roughly how much the item costs in a fixed-price shop and aim to conclude the deal at a slightly lower price than that. In highly touristy areas, the trader may assume you have no idea of the value of an item and ask for far too much in the hope that you'll fall for it. We'd recommend a counter offer of about 50 percent of the vendor's suggestion. Then be prepared to haggle in a friendly manner until you meet in the middle.

Hong Kong is a shoppers' paradise. From traditional

feature. Hong Kong is a great place to buy jade and the tourism board offers online resources detailing how to spot high-quality jade. Flea markets, such as at Cat Street (Upper Lascar Row), offer Mao memorabilia, posters, jewelry and much more.

Chinese Specialties

Ceramics are also an excellent investment. Both Chinese and Western dinnerware, teapots in handmade basket cozies and abstract pottery will provide a beautiful memory of Hong Kong. Chinese cooking utensils are inexpensive to buy in the wetmarkets as are pretty teapots and mugs. Also attractive are bamboo steamer baskets for vegetables and tiffin carriers—stacked metal lunchboxes for taking food to work. Inexpensive and difficult to find outside of Chinese communities are Chinese dried ingredients and herbal remedies such as ginseng, dried fish abalone, and even birds' nests. Chinese tea is also a worthy purchase, with *pu'er* (fermented black tea) and oolong being among the top choices.

For a more modern take on Chinese specialties, check out popular indie shopping centers such as PMQ, the former site of the Police Married Quarters, where you'll find stylish Hong Kong-inspired goods.

Pleasure and Purchase

Among locals shopping is a way of life. For a fun day out, the whole family will visit a shopping center to enjoy the food halls, the air-conditioning and the thrill of a purchase.

Chinese products to international designer stores, this city has it all

SAFE SHOPPING

The Hong Kong Tourist Board lists all the places that have qualified under its Quality Shops and Restaurants scheme on its website. You can check approved members of the scheme at discoverhongkong.com before heading out, or look for the QTS logo displayed on the establishment's window. Be vigilant: Check your package after payment to ensure you've received exactly what you purchased.

Shopping by Theme

Whether you're looking for a department store, a quirky boutique, or something in between, you'll find it all in Hong Kong. On this page, shops are listed by theme. For a more detailed write-up, see the individual listings in Hong Kong by Area.

Hong Kong by Night

Hong Kong Island is the place to head for after-dark excitement. The dining and drinking district of Lan Kwai Fong (LKF) is the most obvious nightlife hub. It's a largely pedestrianized city block, full of buildings that throb with bustling watering holes on the lower floors. The bars tend to be popular with young professionals seeking a night cap after a day at the office. Near to midnight, you'll discover a party atmosphere, with happy tipplers spilling out onto the streets.

Relaxing

To the east, the district of Wan Chai served Hong Kong's red light district during the days of the Vietnam War. Nowadays, it is more respectable, with many reputable live music venues, trendy cocktail bars and low-key eateries. Wan Chai is home to some relaxed pubs if all you want is a quiet drink. With its wine bars, the Star Street precinct, between Wan Chai and Admiralty, is good if you're looking for a slightly more refined evening experience.

Party with the Locals

Kowloon also offers plenty of opportunities to party, especially in Tsim Sha Tsui (TST) where there are many bars and clubs around Knutsford Terrace. The bars generally open around midday and close after 2am, while clubs open from around 6pm until around 1am on weekdays and as late as 4am on the weekends.

There are plenty of bars, clubs and restaurants to try in Hong Kong

HOSTESS CLUBS

Hong Kong developed a racy reputation in the 1960s and 1970s when it became frequented by American soldiers and sailors during the Korea and Vietnam Wars. There are still some traces of Hong Kong's lurid side in the hostess clubs. At times, customers may inadvertently find themselves on the wrong end of a huge bill. Be warned: Though advertised drink prices may sound reasonable, customers may be charged for merely talking to one of the scantily clad service staff.

Where to Eat

Along with shopping, eating is another favorite pastime. Hong Kong has one of the highest per capita ratio of restaurants in the world. Although the city is famed for its Cantonese cuisine, it also has many international and fusion restaurants.

Cantonese Cuisine
Typical Cantonese dishes include crab in black bean sauce, steamed fish, shrimp with chili sauce, roast pigeon and fried noodles with beef. Meals are often accompanied by Chinese tea, the three basic types being black, jasmine and oolong. Needless to say, milk and sugar aren't required.

Where to Eat
Restaurants in the more expensive hotels serve high-quality cuisine, while those on the outlying islands tend to specialize in seafood. Street vendors, though no longer so prevalent, sell a variety of reasonably priced snacks, such as fish balls, noodles and roasted chestnuts. If you are feeling brave, forgo the established restaurants and try your chopstick skills (▷ 50, panel) in one of the tiny street cafés selling pork and rice or wanton noodles (▷ 48, panel).

Opening Hours
Restaurants usually open for lunch around 11.30am, closing at 3pm and then opening again for dinner between 6 and 11pm. A 10 percent service charge is usually added to the bill and additional tips aren't expected in local restaurants.

AFTERNOON TEA

The British ritual of afternoon tea is still going strong in this former colony. For three tiers of delicious treats and all the traditional trimmings, the InterContinental hotel's Lobby Lounge (▷ 112) is hard to beat, however, the Grand Hyatt in Wan Chai and the Mandarin Oriental in Central (▷ 112) are extremely worthy (and equally expensive) alternatives.

Hong Kongers love to eat and the island has both Cantonese and international restaurants to choose from

Where to Eat by Cuisine

There are places to eat to suit all tastes and budgets in Hong Kong. On this page they are listed by cuisine. For a more detailed description of each venue, see Hong Kong by Area.

American and Mexican
Anthony's Ranch (▷ 90)
Bostonian Seafood & Grill (▷ 73)
Mezzo (▷ 75)

Cantonese
The 8 Restaurant (▷ 105)
China Bear (▷ 105)
Dynasty 8 (▷ 105)
Fu Sing (▷ 49)
Jumbo Kingdom (▷ 49)
Man Wah Restaurant (▷ 50)
Maxim's Palace (▷ 50)
Ming Court (▷ 75)
Shang Palace (▷ 106)
Sha Tin 18 (▷ 90)
Yan Toh Heen (▷ 76)
Yung Kee Restaurant (▷ 50)

European
360 Bar, Restaurant & Lounge (▷ 105)
Albergue 1601 (▷ 105)
Ava (▷ 73)
Bathers Restaurant (▷ 105)
Blue (▷ 48)
Caprice (▷ 48)
Harlan's (▷ 75)
Jimmy's Kitchen (▷ 49)
Lobster Bar and Grill (▷ 49)
A Lorcha (▷ 105)
Maze Grill (▷ 75)
The Pawn (▷ 50)
La Terrazza Bar and Grill (▷ 90)

French
Amigo Restaurant (▷ 48)
Brasserie on the Eighth (▷ 48)
Gaddi's (▷ 75)
Rech by Alain Ducasse (▷ 75)
Robuchon au Dome (▷ 106)

Indian
Chaiwala (▷ 48)
Delhi Club (▷ 74)
Gaylord Indian Restaurant (▷ 74)
Goa Nights (▷ 106)
Khyber Pass (▷ 75)
Woodlands International Restaurant (▷ 76)

Italian
Aqua Roma (▷ 73)
Theo Mistral by Theo Randall (▷ 76)

Japanese
Aqua Tokyo (▷ 73)
Nadaman (▷ 75)
Sagano Restaurant (▷ 76)
Sakurada (▷ 90)
Shikigiku Japanese Restaurant (▷ 76)
Tokio Joe (▷ 50)

Pan-Asian
Felix (▷ 74)
Fu Lum Fusion (▷ 90)
Indonesian Restaurant 1968 (▷ 49)
Peak Café Bar (▷ 50)
Tung Kee Seafood Restaurant (▷ 90)

Sichuan
Haidilao (▷ 106)

Spanish
El Cid (▷ 48)
El Loco Gringo (▷ 49)

Taiwanese
Din Tai Fung (▷ 74)

Vegetarian
Ah Por Tofu Fa (▷ 90)
Green Common (▷ 74)

ESSENTIAL HONG KONG WHERE TO EAT BY CUISINE

Top Tips For…

These suggestions will help plan an ideal visit to Hong Kong, no matter how you choose to spend your time. Each sight or listing has a fuller write-up elsewhere in the book.

ISLAND HOPPING
Spend a day relaxing on Cheung Chau island (▷ 94–95) dining on fresh seafood or lazing on the beach.
Get away from traffic on Lamma (▷ 98) with seafood restaurants, bars and beaches.
Soar above Lantau (▷ 96–97) on the shiny Ngong Ping 360 cable car to see the giant Buddha.
Take a trip out to tiny Po Toi (▷ 99) for challenging treks and to see the island's ancient rock carvings.

PAMPERING
Soothe your stress with a mudbath and massage at the Four Seasons Spa (▷ 112).
Enjoy a traditional Chinese massage at Cordis, Hong Kong (▷ 112) in Mong Kok.
Try reflexology and aromatherapy, then unwind in a sauna at the Island Shangri-La (▷ 112).

SHOPPING MALLS
Indulge in a little retail therapy at the Harbour City malls (▷ 70).
Check out the luxury goods at the "canalside" Sands Shoppes, Macau (▷ 104).
Cool down with some ice skating at naturally lit Festival Walk rink (▷ 70).

SKYSCRAPERS
Tell the time using the roof of Central Plaza (▷ 40).
Check out the amazing architecture of the inside-out Hong Kong & Shanghai Banking Corporation Building (▷ 41).
Wonder at the stylish 72-story Bank of China Tower (▷ 40) with its mixture of Ming dynasty and ultramodern design.

Clockwise from top left: Spa pampering; browsing the Stanley Market; Man Mo Temple; a luxurious

MARKETS

Take the bus out to Stanley (▷ 32–33) where the market fills the town.

Refresh your wardrobe with inexpensive clothes at the Ladies' Market (▷ 70).

Browse the packed "lanes" of Li Yuen Street Market, one of Hong Kong's oldest street markets, for accessories and souvenirs (▷ 45).

Buy a piece of jade and try the seafood at Temple Street Night Market (▷ 64).

TEMPLES

Meet Taoist gods Man and Mo at the name-sake temple (▷ 29).

Have your fortune read by a professional at the huge Wong Tai Sin Temple (▷ 84).

Count the Buddha statues at the Ten Thousand Buddhas Monastery (▷ 82–83).

Visit the interesting 18th-century Stanley temple dedicated to Tin Hau, the goddess of seafarers (▷ 32).

PARTYING

Dance the night away in the Wan Chai's district's hedonistic bars and clubs (▷ 46).

Hang out with cool cats at Castro's (▷ 72).

Enjoy the after-work vibe among Hong Kong's professional set at Staunton's (▷ 47).

Experience a cocktail with a view at stylish Sevva (▷ 47).

ROOMS WITH A VIEW

Request a room with a view of the harbor at the InterContinental (▷ 112).

Gaze down from one of Hong Kong's highest guestrooms in the Ritz-Carlton (▷ 112).

Peer over skyscraper roofs from the Island Shangri-La tower (▷ 112).

Explore the heart of Mong Kok from a home-base at Cordis, Hong Kong (112).

Watch the pulse of the city by day and by night from a room at the beautifully, and recently, refurbished Mandarin Oriental (112).

Eat your heart out at the Four Seasons' lineup of all-star restaurants (112).

harbor-view room at the Island Shangri-La; skyscrapers of Central district; Sevva roof terrace

STROLLS IN THE PARK

Check out the beautiful, but man-made, splendors of Hong Kong Park (▷ 28).

See trees, plants and animals from around the world at the Zoological and Botanical Gardens (▷ 42).

Admire the statues, bird life and landscaped ponds of Kowloon Park (▷ 67).

Enjoy the remains of the notorious Kowloon Walled City in the eponymous park (▷ 56).

USING CHOPSTICKS

Exercise your digits at the Jumbo Kingdom (▷ 49).

Grapple with dim sum dishes (▷ panel, 48) using traditional chopsticks (▷ panel, 50).

Dig into some traditional Cantonese cuisine at Yung Kee Restaurant (▷ 50).

ENTERTAINING THE KIDS

See the pandas and enjoy the rides at Ocean Park (▷ 31).

Meet the orangutans at the Zoological Gardens (▷ 42).

Take a sampan ride around Aberdeen Harbour (▷ 24–25).

Get hands-on at the Hong Kong Science Museum (▷ 57).

WHAT'S FREE

Climb to the top of The Peak and admire the amazing views from the roof of the Peak Galleria Mall (▷ 38–39).

Enjoy the exhibits at the University Museum and Art Gallery (▷ 36–37).

Goggle at the Symphony of Lights each evening (▷ 62–63).

Ride the escalator to the Mid Levels to get a feel for SoHo, Hong Kong's nightlife and dining district (▷ 30).

Spend a day at Silverstrand beach up north in Sai Kung (▷ 89).

Explore Tai Kwun, a 19th-century police headquarters revamped into a lifestyle and arts hub on Wyndham Street (▷ 34–35).

From top: the Zoological and Botanical Gardens; Chinese chopsticks; a sea lion at Ocean Park; view from the Peak

Hong Kong by Area

From shopping malls to sandy beaches, temples to theme parks, haute cuisine to dim sum, and designer labels to souvenirs, Hong Kong Island has it all.

Top 25

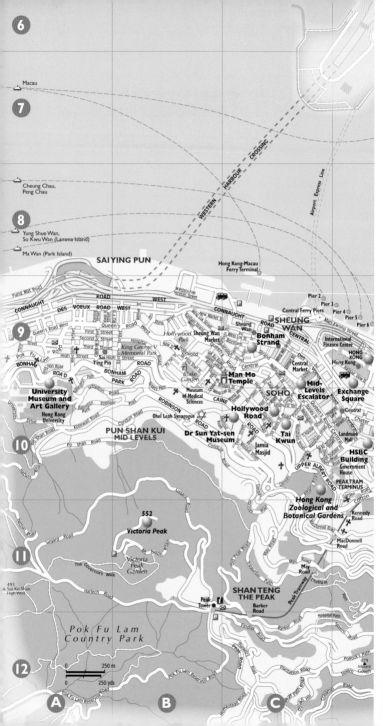

6

7

Macau

Cheung Chau,
Peng Chau

8

Yung Shue Wan,
So Kwu Wan (Lamma Island)

Ma Wan (Park Island)

SAI YING PUN

Hong Kong-Macau
Ferry Terminal

HARBOUR CROSSING

WESTERN

Airport Express Line

Pier 2

Central Ferry Piers

Pier 3
Pier 4
Pier 5
Pier 6

Man Kwong Street

SHEUNG WAN
CENTRAL

CONNAUGHT ROAD

CONNAUGHT ROAD WEST

DES VOEUX ROAD WEST

Western Fire Services Street

New Market Street

Queen's Road West

First Street
Second Street
Third Street
Sai High Street
Ying Pin

Hollywood Park

Sheung Wan Market

Bonham Strand

9

Fung Mat Road

Queen's Road West

Pok Fu Lam

BONHAM ROAD

King George V
Memorial Park

Hospital Path

Hollywood Road

New Street

Queen's Road Central

Central

International
Finance Centre

HONG
KONG

Hong Kong

University
Museum and
Art Gallery

Hong Kong
University

BONHAM ROAD

PARK ROAD

Babington Path

Lyttleton Road

ROBINSON ROAD

Ohel Leah Synagogue

Blake
Garden

Museum
of Medical
Sciences

CAINE ROAD

Man Mo
Temple

SOHO

Central
Market

Mid-
Levels
Escalator

Exchange
Square

Central   Chater

Landmark
Mall

University Drive

Kotewall Road

Conduit Road

Po Shan Road

PUN SHAN KUI
MID LEVELS

Po Shan Road

Dr Sun Yat-sen
Museum

Hollywood Road

Jamia
Masjid

ROBINSON ROAD

Tai
Kwun

Conduit Road

UPPER ALBERT ROAD

HSBC
Building

Government
House

PEAK TRAM
TERMINUS

10

Hatton Road

Hatton Road

Lung Fu Shan
Road

Hong Kong
Zoological and
Botanical Gardens

Garden Road

Cotton Tree Drive

Kennedy
Road

MacDonnell
Road

552
Victoria Peak

Mt Austin Road

Lugard Road

Harlech Road

Victoria
Peak
Garden

The Governor's Walk

Hospital Path

Severn Road

Plantation Road

May Road

May Road

Chatham Path

Peak Tramway

11

493
Sai Kn Shan
High Wind

Lugard Road

Harlech Road

SHAN TENG
THE PEAK

Barker Road

Peak
Tower

Barker Road

Findlay Road

Hospital Path

Pok Fu Lam
Country Park

Peak Road

Plantation Road

Pollock's Path

479
Mount
Gough

12

0   250 m

0   250 yds

Pok Fu Lam Reservoir Road

Pok Fu Lam Reservoir Road

Peel Rise

Guildford Road

Severn Road

A

B

C

Victoria   Harbour

Pier 7
Pier 8   Hong Kong
Maritime Museum
Pier 9
The Hong Kong
Observation Wheel
Pier 10
Two IFC

CHUNG WAN
CENTRAL DISTRICT

City Hall
HARCOURT
Statue
Square
Chater
Garden
Central
Government
Offices
Former
Legislative
Council
Building
Bank of
China
Tower
Admiralty
St John's
Cathedral
Flagstaff House
Museum of Tea Ware
Harcourt
Garden

Hong Kong Convention and
Exhibition Centre
Convention Avenue   Hung Hom Road
Convention
Harbour Road
Central
Plaza
HARBOUR   ROAD
GLOUCESTER

WAN
CHAI

Hong Kong Academy
for Performing Arts
HARCOURT ROAD

Jaffe   Road
Lockhart   Road   HENNESSY   ROAD
HENNESSY   ROAD   Wan Chai
Thomson   Road
JOHNSTON   ROAD

Hong Kong
Park

Kennedy   Road

QUEEN'S   ROAD   EAST

Tai Wong
Temple

Bowen   Road

Sikh
Temple

Muslim
Cemetery

Hong Kong
Cemetery

MAGAZINE
GAP

Pak Tai
Temple

STUBBS

ROAD

Police
Museum

PEAK   ROAD

STUBBS   ROAD

Black's Link

HONG KONG
ISLAND

Mount Nicholson Road

D   **E**   **F**

Aberdeen

HIGHLIGHTS

● Dinner at the Jumbo Kingdom (▷ 49)
● A sampan ride around the harbor
● Views over the harbor from the Chinese cemetery above the town

TIP

● Ap Lei Chau has become a hot spot of outlets where anything from last year's designer clothing to furniture and antiques at low prices can be found.

Before the British arrived, Aberdeen was a small village, full of pirates and fishermen. Today the pirates are gone, but fishing remains the livelihood of many families.

Fragrant Harbor Aberdeen is known in Chinese as Heung Gong Tsai, meaning "little fragrant harbor;" this name is thought to have derived from the village's trade in sandalwood and incense production. The whole of the Special Administrative Region (SAR) of Hong Kong is described by this term. The chief draw of a visit to Aberdeen is to tour the harbor where, for centuries, families have lived their lives on houseboats all moored tightly together. At the western end of the harbor is the city's longest running wholesale fish market.

Aberdeen harbor is full of life, being home to a large fishing fleet and hundreds of people living on junks. It is renowned for its floating restaurants, of which the most famous is the Jumbo Floating Restaurant–with a staff of more than 300

Highlights A highlight of your visit is to negotiate with one of the savvy old ladies that ply tourists around the harbor. Starting from Aberdeen Fishing Village, take a trip out to Ap Lei Chau (around HK$50), a tiny island just offshore. The 28-floor Horizon Plaza, on Lee Wing Street, is great for discounted fashions and reproductions. Back in Aberdeen, the Tin Hau Temple dedicated to the goddess of the sea, on Reservoir Road, is worth a look, followed by a walk uphill to the huge cemetery with views over the harbor.

Floating restaurants There are two mega-restaurants in Aberdeen harbor catering to the vast numbers of people who come here for the seafood. Free ferries take customers to the restaurants, which are adjacent to each other.

THE BASICS

➕ See map ▷ 92–93
✉ Aberdeen
🍴 The two floating restaurants of Jumbo Kingdom, bars and cafés in town
🚌 70 from Exchange Square
♿ Few
✋ Sampan boats: inexpensive

Flagstaff House
Museum of Tea Ware

TOP 25

The Museum of Tea Ware is housed in an elegant white building in Hong Kong Park

THE BASICS

hk.art.museum
🔁 E11
✉ 10 Cotton Tree Drive, Central
☎ 2869 0690
🕐 Wed–Mon 10–5
🍴 Nearby cafés
🚇 Admiralty
♿ Good
🖐 Free

HIGHLIGHTS

● Graceful Greek Rival grandeur
● Rare ceramics and antiques
● Hands-on tea tasting demonstrations

Completed in 1984, the Flagstaff House Museum of Tea Ware promises hands-on demonstrations, exhibitions and historic galleries amidst the 19th-century architecture.

Majestic architecture As you approach the Flagstaff House of Museum and Tea Ware, the first thing you'll notice is the beautiful white facade. Built in the 1940s, the grand manor was once home to the commander of the British forces, beginning with Major-General G. C. D'Aguilar in 1844, and followed by a string of successors. As the oldest colonial building remaining in Hong Kong, this prestigious address sports graceful Greek Revival verandahs and ogle-worthy columns.

Tea through the ages Inside, the exhibition of colorful teapots could bring out the collector in almost anyone. Dating from 1984, the tea ware galleries provide an extensive introduction to Hong Kong's rich tea culture. The extensive exhibitions include ancient ceramic artwork dating to the 7th century BC, calligraphy, stone carvings and free explanatory workshops regarding tea culture.

Time for tea In addition to the exhibitions you can also take part in one of the regular tea-preparation demonstrations or informative lectures. Cap off the morning with a visit to famous Lock Cha Tea House, housed inside the museum's K. S. Lo Gallery.

Happy Valley Racecourse

Horse racing has long been a staple in Hong Kong, having emerged in the 1840s during British rule to satisfy the whims of the rich and the aristocracy. These days, Wednesday nights at the races are a casual, fun-filled affair for all comers.

Jaw-dropping scenery Surrounded by bright lights and skyscrapers, the lush green Happy Valley track provides a fabulous setting for a mid-week night. The racing season runs from about September to July. The most anticipated race of the year is the LONGINES Hong Kong International Race, which takes place in December and brings together top riders from around the world to compete for a HK$93 million purse. In terms of domestic races, the BMW Hong Kong Derby, which usually takes place in March, is another highlight of the equestrian calendar.

History awaits For more than 150 years Hong Kong has embraced the so-called sport of Kings, and that passion continues today. The Hong Kong Jockey Club opened the Happy Valley racetrack in 1884. For some time, the races were only accessible by the city's elite—most of whom were British expatriates. These days, however, the races are open to all, and all of the HK$3 billion of the Jockey Club's annual profits go toward charity. When the Happy Valley course reached capacity by the 1970s, the Club opened a second track, this time in Sha Tin, to sate the city's racing zeal.

THE BASICS

happywednesday.hkjc.com

G11

2 Sports Road, Happy Valley

2895 1523

Wednesday 5.15pm–11pm

Causeway Bay

1, 10 from Central; Happy Valley Tram

Snack kiosks, Beer Garden, The Gallery

Good

Inexpensive

HIGHLIGHTS

● Views from the second floor terrace
● Season Opening Day: the first Wednesday in September
● Digital betting machines

Hong Kong Park

TOP 25

Plants and birds in the aviary at Hong Kong Park

THE BASICS

lcsd.gov.hk/parks/hkp

⊕ D11

✉ Main entrance: Supreme Court Road, Central. Nearest entrance to Museum of Teaware: Cotton Tree Drive, Central

☎ Museum: 2869 0690

🕐 Park: 6am–11pm. Museum: Wed–Mon 10–5. Aviary and Conservatory 9–5. Closed 24–25 Dec, 1 Jan and first 3 days of Chinese New Year

🍴 Café/bar in park

🚇 Admiralty

🚌 12, 23B, 40, 103; get off at first stop in Cotton Tree Drive

♿ Good

✋ Free

HIGHLIGHTS

● Walk-in aviary
● Artificial waterfalls
● Conservatory
● Observation tower
● Bonsai and Banyan trees
● Hong Kong Zoological and Botanical Gardens (▷ 42)

In a space-deprived Hong Kong, this modern park is a joy. Instead of roses or trees you'll find man-made waterfalls, concrete pools and meandering paths around the grass and flowers, providing a sense of harmony and balance.

Artificial paradise Hong Kong's city planners and architects built this park into the contours of the hillside. It's fun to walk past the pools filled with koi carp or go through the Edward Youde Aviary, where tree-high walkways take you cheek-by-bill with brightly plumaged tropical birds.

The conservatory The Forsgate Conservatory is an enormous building. It has three separate sections—display plants, humid plants and dry plants—which take up a large chunk of the entire park. Adjustable climate control equipment simulates conditions from disparate regions, and the many varieties of bamboo are particularly impressive.

Peaceful oasis Early in the morning the gardens are full of people performing t'ai chi, a martial art commonly practiced in Hong Kong for general health and self defense. You might also cross paths with avid runners and fitness groups, who use the public space for stair-running, interval training, and even weight lifting. But there's no need to break a sweat here—enjoy the peace and quiet whenever you need a break from the frenetic city streets.

The altar (left) and Man Mo incense coils (right)

Man Mo Temple

The most remarkable aspect of this tiny but historic temple is the canopy of incense coils which creates a heady, mysterious atmosphere.

Taoism The temple, built in 1847, is one of the oldest surviving structures on Hong Kong Island and looks rather bullied by the soaring apartment blocks that surround it. It is dedicated to two Taoist deities who represent the pen and the sword. These are Man, or Man Cheong, the god of literature; and Mo, or Kuan Ti, the god of war. The statues of Man and Mo are dressed lavishly in beautifully embroidered outfits. Beside the two main statues are representations of Pao Kung, the god of justice, and Shing Wong, the god who protects this region of the city. By the door are the figures of some lesser deities. A drum and a gong are sounded whenever an offering is made to the gods. The atmosphere seems casual—cats wander around, fortune-tellers divine the future using *chim* (numbered bamboo sticks), and visitors place offerings of fruit or incense sticks in the offering boxes inside the temple.

Nearby sights Next door, to the right, is the Lit Shing Kung, or All Saints Temple. Here, too, you can see people consulting resident soothsayers, who interpret the *chim* tipped out of bamboo pots. In the courtyard of the temple stand gilded plaques, carried in processions, while inside are the two 1862 sedan chairs used to convey the figures of the two gods.

THE BASICS

man-mo-temple.hk
🕇 C9
✉ 124–126 Hollywood Road (near Ladder Street)
🕐 Daily 8–6
🚇 Sheung Wan
🚌 26
♿ Access difficult
🎫 Free

HIGHLIGHTS

● Statues of Man Cheong and Kuan Ti
● Sedan chairs once used to carry the statues
● Embroideries surrounding the statues
● Drum and bell on right of entrance door
● Soot-blackened deities on left of entrance door
● Gold and brass standards carried during parades
● Resident fortune-tellers

Mid-Levels Escalator

TOP 25

Mid-Levels Escalator in the Central Area, and SoHo District (right)

THE BASICS

➕ C10
✉ 100 Queens Road Central, Central
🕐 Daily 6am–midnight
🍴 Gage Street, Staunton Street
Ⓜ Central
♿ Poor

HIGHLIGHTS

- Central Market building
- Gage Street
- Graham Street
- Tai Kwun
- SoHo
- Jamia Mosque

The world's longest outdoor escalator system runs to 2,625ft (800m), and comprises 20 distinct sections.

Up Built in the early 1990s to ease traffic congestion in the narrow streets below, the (officially named) Central Mid-Levels Escalator has had the effect of breathing new life into whole swathes of Central. Used by around 78,000 pedestrians each day, it operates downhill until 10am and uphill thereafter, easing the commute for the area's salarymen and women.

Down The escalator starts at 100 Queen's Road Central, emerging from next to the Central Market building. This 1930s Bauhaus building sits on the site of Hong Kong's oldest colonial market, established in 1842. The route then takes walkers up Cochrane Street, across Hollywood Road to Shelley Street and then on to Conduit Road, high in the Mid Levels.

All around Notable streets en route include Hollywood Road, a haven for collectors of art and antiques. There's a great view from here of Tai Kwun, a heritage revitalization project that has transformed the former Central Police Station into a lifestyle mecca. Descend here and head to Graham Street and one of Hong Kong's best outdoor markets. The streets beyond Hollywood Road, commonly known as SoHo, have been reborn as a drinking and dining hub thanks to the elevator. Beyond, near the top of the escalator, is the Jamia Mosque.

Ocean Park

Wildlife, history, scenic views, arts and crafts, and animal shows—not to mention exciting rides—make up this park.

Thrills galore There is so much to see and do at this park that it takes a little time to plan your visit. Identify times and locations of the animal shows and organize your day around them.

Aerial view The park is organized into two main sections: rollercoasters and animal attractions. The lowland section is called The Waterfront, while the upland section is The Summit. Transit between the two is by foot on Hong Kong's second-longest outdoor escalator system, by funicular railway the "Ocean Express," or, best of all, the cable car, which has views over the park and sea.

What to see Ocean Park is home to two Giant Pandas. The young pandas—Le Le and Ying Ying—arrived as babies in 2007 and can be found in the Giant Panda Adventure area. The Grand Aquarium, which is home to more than 400 species of fish, has a multi-level walk-through tank. At the summit is Marine World, Games Zone (with over 20 classic arcade games) and the Ocean Park Tower, which rotates passengers at a height of 236ft (72m).

Rides Both areas have rides and some stomach-churning rollercoasters, though younger children may prefer the Whiskers Harbour zone in the park's Waterfront section.

THE BASICS

oceanpark.com.hk

⊞ See map ▷ 92–93

✉ Ocean Park Road, Aberdeen

☎ 3923 2323

🕐 Daily 10–8

🍴 Fastfood, Bayview Restaurant Terrace Café

🚍 MTR, Citibus 629 leaves from Admiralty MTR every 10 min and leaves the Star Ferry Terminal every 20–60 min

♿ Excellent

💰 Expensive

❓ Height restrictions on some rides

HIGHLIGHTS

● The Grand Aquarium
● Ocean Theatre animal shows
● Raging River flume ride
● Pandas Le Le and Ying Ying
● Emperors of the Sky bird show
● Dragon Ride and Hair Raiser

Stanley

HIGHLIGHTS

● Views from bus to
Stanley
● Tin Hau Temple
● Stanley Beach
● St. Stephen's Beach
● Stanley Military
Cemetery
● Stanley Market (▷ 45)
● Kuan Yin Temple

TIPS

● A 15-minute walk along
Wong Ma Kok Road is a
signpost down to the much
quieter St. Stephen's Beach.
● Check out the
Correctional Services
Museum at 45 Tung Tau
Wan Road (Tue–Sun 10–5).
Admission is free.

**The most stunning thing about a visit
to Stanley, on the south side of Hong
Kong Island, is the journey there. Get an
upstairs seat on the double-decker bus—
the ride is as good as any at Ocean Park.**

Temples Most visitors come to Stanley for
its market, but the village has many other
attractions. Close to the market is the Tin Hau
Temple, first built on this spot in the early
1700s. The bell and drum are said to have
belonged to a famous pirate, Cheung Po-Tsai.
The bell was cast in 1767, and it is thought
that the pirate used it to send messages to his
ships. The temple also contains the skin of a
tiger, shot in Stanley in 1942. Farther along the
road is a second temple, dedicated to Kuan Yin,
goddess of mercy. Some claim to have seen
the 20ft (6m) statue of the goddess move.

Visit Stanley for its market, beaches and temples, or just for a walk along the seafront

Beaches and the market The beach at Stanley is a good one, and a short bus ride farther along takes you to St. Stephen's Beach, where there is a graveyard for all the soldiers who have died in Hong Kong since Britain claimed the island as a colony. Although now rather touristy, the famous market is quite good, with linen shops as well as posters, paintings, ceramics and fresh juice vendors. Stanley is the stepping-off point for Po Toi Island (▷ 99), an hour's ferry ride away, but worth the trip for the prehistoric rock carvings, delicious calamari at a local restaurant and a good beach for swimming.

The three-story Murray House was relocated, stone-by-stone, from Central, where it was formerly a British Army barracks dating to 1848. It houses several restaurants, replete with verandahs and terraces with sea views.

THE BASICS

✚ See map ▷ 92–93
🕐 Market 10.30–6.30. Temple 6–6
🍴 Restaurants and pub food in Stanley Main Street
🚌 6, 6A, 6X, 66, 260 from Exchange Square
⛴ Ferries to Po Toi depart Sat 1.20pm, Sun 10am, 11.30am, 3.30pm and 5pm
♿ Excellent

Tai Kwun

HIGHLIGHTS

● Incredible architecture
● A rare, wide-open courtyard
● Local artwork and performances

TIP

● The easiest way to reach Tai Kwun is via the Central Mid-Levels Escalator to the direct entrance from the walkway, right after you cross Hollywood Road. For barrier-free access, use the Bauhinia House Gate.

As Hong Kong's largest-ever revitalization project, Tai Kwun touched down in the former Central Police Station in 2018. The colonial-era architecture provides an old-world setting for the heritage, arts and modern lifestyle complex.

An architectural feat Sponsored by the Hong Kong Jockey Club, the mammoth scheme took more than eight years and some HK$3.8 billion to complete. But the result is breathtaking: More than 16 heritage buildings, including the former Victoria Prison, the Barrack Block and the Central Magistracy have been reimagined as restaurants, art galleries, theaters and chic fashion boutiques. Swiss studio Herzog de Meuron led the meticulous, and sympathetic, restoration process.

Tai Kwun brings together contemporary art, dining and fashion within the former 20th-century Central Police Station compound

Artsy experience Set in the heart of Central along Wyndham Street, Tai Kwun is a must-visit for arts and culture lovers. On site, you'll find several galleries, exhibition spaces and performing arts venues that feature a multitude of work by local and regional talents. Next door, the ultramodern JC Contemporary Gallery juxtaposes the Victorian-style redbrick former police compound and turns a spotlight on the city's eclectic architecture.

Dining destination You will also find a slew of restaurants and bars inside the complex, including the uber-photogenic Madame Fu's for Chinese, Ashley Sutton's whimsical Dragonfly bar, The Chinese Library and David Thompson's Aaharn, marking the celebrity chef's Hong Kong debut.

THE BASICS
taikwun.hk
✚ C10
✉ 10 Hollywood Road, Central
☎ 3559 2600
⏰ Daily 11–11
🍴 Restaurants, bars, fast food
🚌 Central
♿ Excellent
✋ Free

University Museum and Art Gallery

HIGHLIGHTS

● Nestorian bronze crosses
● Bronze mirrors
● Neolithic black pottery cup
● Pottery horse, Western Han dynasty
● Qing dynasty woodcarving
● Bronze drum
● Sui dynasty spittoons
● Indian Buddhist sculptures
● Modern Chinese pottery from Jinghdezhen and Shiwan

TIP

● The Tea Gallery serves tea in the traditional style: Mon–Sat 10–5, Sun 2–5.

A must-see for history buffs, The University of Hong Kong's Museum and Art Gallery houses an extensive collection of Chinese art and culture artifacts.

Nestorian bronze crosses The hidden treasures beautifully displayed in this out-of-the-way museum, in the university's Fung Ping Shan Building, date from the 5th century BC onward, but the highlight is a set of 467 Nestorian bronze crosses. They belonged to a Christian sect that originated in Syria and came to China during the Tang dynasty (AD618–906). The crosses date back to the Yuan dynasty (1280–1367) and were probably worn as part of a belt or as a pendant. They were made in various cross-shapes, including swastikas, birds and conventional crucifixes.

Since its foundation in 1953, the University Museum has amassed over 1,000 Chinese antiquities including bronze rice sculptures, a globe and wooden shutters

Ceramics and bronzes Notable among the many bronze items on display are mirrors from the Warring States period (475–221BC), and Shang and Zhou ritual vessels as well as weapons. The museum also houses an enormous collection of ceramics dating back as far as neolithic times. Look for the three-color glaze Tang pottery items, the famous kiln wares from the Song dynasty and the many polychrome ceramics from the Ming and Qing dynasties.

Beyond Hong Kong Objects from other Asian countries include a selection of Indian Buddhist sculptures and items from Thailand, Vietnam and Korea. Scroll paintings, inlaid blackwood furniture and a huge bronze drum make up the rest of the collection.

THE BASICS

hku.hk/hkumag

➕ A9

✉ 90 Bonham Road

☎ 2241 5500

🕐 Mon–Sat 9.30–6, Sun 1–6. Closed public holidays

🚇 HKU Station Exit A1

🚌 3B from City Hall on Connaught Road or 23, 40, 40M from Pacific Place, Admiralty

♿ None

🆓 Free

Victoria Peak

HIGHLIGHTS

- Views over Hong Kong
- Tram ride to the top
- Old Governor's Lodge, with toposcope in its gardens
- Souvenirs in Peak Galleria
- Circular walk around Lugard and Harlech roads
- Green-arrowed walk up Mount Austin Road

TIPS

- If you can, head to The Peak on a clear day.
- Take a picnic and do the walk around Circle Walk.

Visiting The Peak is one of the first things you should do on a trip to Hong Kong. At 1,811ft (552m), the hilltop views are spectacular and the area offers some peaceful, shady walks.

Head for heights Some people like to make the pilgrimage up The Peak twice—once during the day and again at night to see the city lights. Both are worthwhile, but Hong Kong's regular haze makes a night-time visit the safest bet if time is short. The Peak is a relatively unspoiled oasis in a concrete jungle, and a good place for a quiet walk.

Top stop The Peak Tower offers multiple distractions, including a Madame Tussauds and heaps of touristy shops. The highlight is the Sky

The best thing about The Peak is its breathtaking views over the city. The Peak Tower (bottom right) was designed by British architect Terry Farrell in the shape of an upheld rice bowl

Terrace 428, a ticketed 360-degree viewing platform which boasts a panoramic view over Central, the harbor and Kowloon beyond. If you don't want to pay, the Circle Walk around the mountain via Lugard and Harlech roads offers arguably even better views and will take less than an hour. Across the square from the Peak Tower is the Peak Galleria with its simple terrace and many restaurants and shops.

View from the top The trip up in The Peak Tram, constructed in 1888, is good fun, but avoid weekends and the first day after a misty spell. From the tram stop you can walk along Mount Austin Road to Victoria Park Gardens and the ruins of the Governor's Lodge, destroyed by the Japanese in World War II. A noticeboard displays the hour-long walk routes.

THE BASICS

thepeak.com.hk

⊞ B11

✉ Peak Tower, Peak Road

⏱ Peak Tram: runs 7am–midnight

🍴 Cafés and restaurants

🚋 Trams run every 10–15 min from terminals at Garden Road and Cotton Tree Drive. Route 15 from Exchange Square

♿ Good

💷 Tram fare: moderate. Sky Terrace 428: moderate. Peak Tower: free

More to See

BANK OF CHINA TOWER

bochk.com

Designed by the Chinese-American architect I. M. Pei, and constructed between 1985 and 1990, this 1,205-ft (367m) high, 70-floor tower stands out amid the Hong Kong skyline. The building soars upward in a series of triangles toward a prism at the top. There is a 43rd-floor viewing platform (free), open Monday to Saturday.

🔡 D10 🖂 No. 1 Garden Road, Central
🕐 Mon–Fri 8–6 🚇 Central 🎟 Free

BONHAM STRAND

Ginseng shops, antiques markets and tiny lanes with old-school dried seafood now abound on the road where the British first set foot. Despite the renovations, this area still recalls the old Hong Kong and many traditions persist.

🔡 C9 🖂 Bonham Strand, Sheung Wan
🕐 Shops close on public holidays, Chinese New Year 🍴 Food stalls in Sheung Wan Market and streets around Bonham Strand; fast food near MTR station 🚇 Sheung Wan

🚋 Trams stop at Western Market and go on through Central to Causeway Bay 🅿 Good
🎟 Free

CAUSEWAY BAY

This district is famous for fashion and rowdy local restaurants. It's particularly fun at night. It's home to the excellent Central Library as well as Happy Valley Racecourse.

🔡 H9 🍴 Many 🚇 Causeway Bay
🅿 Good

CENTRAL PLAZA

centralplaza.com.hk

This office block deserves a visit for stunning views from the Sky Lobby on the 46th floor. Completed in 1992, Central Plaza stands at 1,227ft (374m)—counting the spire. It is no longer one of Hong Kong's tallest buildings, but it's home to one of the highest churches in the world, located on the 75th floor.

🔡 F10 🖂 18 Harbour Road, Wan Chai
☎ 2586 8111 🍴 Nearby cafés 🚇 Wan Chai 🅿 Good 🎟 Free

Early morning t'ai chi in Victoria Park, Causeway Bay

CHATER GARDEN

Chater Garden is a slice of tropical repose amid the bustling city. Once the site of the Hong Kong Cricket Club and its manicured lawn, the garden is surrounded by a clutch of Central's most iconic skyscrapers—the Bank of China Tower among them. Nearby you'll find Hong Kong's Cenotaph.

🔳 D10 ✉ Between Chater Road and Des Voeux Road ⏰ 24 hours 🚇 Central 🚾 Good

DR. SUN YAT-SEN MUSEUM

hk.drsunyatsen.museum

The arrival in Hong Kong of a museum detailing the life of Sun Yat-Sen feels like confirmation that Hong Kong is back in mainland hands. The revered nationalist leader has museums dedicated to him in several major Chinese cities, but this one, in the 1914 Kom Tong Hall, stands out among the many, both in terms of the architecture and its excellent permanent exhibitions.

🔳 C10 ✉ 7 Castle Road, Mid Levels, Central ☎ 2367 6373 ⏰ Mon–Wed and Fri–Sat 10–6, Sun 10–7 🚌 3B, 12, 23, 40 to Caine 💷 Inexpensive

EXCHANGE SQUARE

Bounded by three ultramodern tower blocks, including the Hong Kong Stock Exchange, the square is linked via a series of overhead walkways to the Sheung Wan district. On Sundays, and without the background hustle of weekday commerce, it becomes a place of quiet contemplation.

🔳 D9 🍴 Café and fast-food outlets 🚇 Exchange Square, Central 🚾 Good

HOLLYWOOD ROAD

If you are a serious antiques collector or just like browsing curios, then head to Hollywood Road. The antiques shops start at the beginning of the road and continue for about 1 mile (1.6km), incorporating Upper Lascar Row. Antiques that are more than 100 years old must have a certificate of authenticity. If you plan on spending a lot, you might want to check with your consulate first to find out if there will be duty charges.

🔳 C10 🚇 Sheung Wan 🚾 Poor

HONG KONG CONVENTION & EXHIBITION CENTRE (HKCEC)

hkcec.com

The once-bland Convention & Exhibition Centre, originally built in 1988 on reclaimed land, underwent extensive expansion in 1997. The new structure has made an iconic impact on the Island's waterfront, being easily identified as the gargantuan spaceship-like building protruding into the harbor. The linked towers of the HKCEC contain two of the Island's most prestigious hotels—the Grand Hyatt and the Renaissance Harbour View. The adjacent Reunification Monument attracts many visitors.

🔳 F10 ✉ 1 Convention Avenue, Wan Chai ☎ 2582 8888 🚇 Wan Chai 💷 Free

HONG KONG & SHANGHAI BANKING CORPORATION (HSBC) BUILDING

This 1985 building, designed by British architect Sir Norman Foster and prefabricated in several continents at a cost of over US$1 billion, looks as if it's been turned inside

out. The supporting structures appear on the outside, mechanical parts are exposed, and many walls are glass. There is public access to the impressive main lobby.

➕ D10 ✉ Des Voeux Road/Statue Square, Central 🚇 Central 🎫 Free

HONG KONG ZOOLOGICAL AND BOTANICAL GARDENS

lcsd.gov.hk/parks

These gardens are a natural wonderland and are home to more than 1,000 plant species. The zoo has a successful endangered-species breeding program, including such animals as the ring-tailed lemur and two-toed sloth.

➕ C10 ✉ From Central use Upper Albert Road entrance ☎ 2530 0154 🕐 Daily 5am–7pm 🚇 Central 🎫 Free

REPULSE BAY

The pretty beach gets very crowded on public holidays and weekends, but is worth the trip. There is a temple as well as The Pulse, a modern shopping and dining center.

Zoological and Botanical Gardens

➕ See map ▷ 92–93 🚌 6, 61 from Central Bus Terminus

ST. JOHN'S CATHEDRAL

stjohnscathedral.org.hk

This Anglican church, a relic of British colonialism, has stood since 1849. The dominant feature inside is the stained-glass representation of the crucifixion. The church can be found below the Lower Peak tram terminal on Garden Road.

➕ D10 ✉ 4-8 Garden Road ☎ 2523 4157 🕐 7–6 🚇 Central ♿ None

STATUE SQUARE

The highlight of this historic square is the neoclassical former Legislative Council (Legco) Building. Built in 1912, it now houses Hong Kong's Court of Final Appeal.

➕ D10 ✉ Between Chater Road and Des Voeux Road Central 🕐 24 hours 🚇 Central ♿ Excellent 🎫 Free

TWO IFC

hkma.gov.hk

Two IFC is a monument dedicated to Hong Kong's post-colonial prosperity. Designed by architect César Pelli, it rises to 1,362ft (415m) spread over "88" floors. Eight is a lucky number across China, and "double eight" more so—the Hong Kong Monetary Authority's chief executive has an office on the 88th floor. Public access is limited, but there's a public museum on the 55th floor with great views. Downstairs is a luxury mall and the Airport Express train occupies the basement.

➕ D9 ✉ 1 Harbour View Street, Central HKMA Info Centre ☎ 2878 1111 🕐 Mon–Fri 10–6, Sat 10–1 🎫 Free

An Island Walk

This inner city walk passes shops selling all manner of herbal remedies, then continues along famous Hollywood Road to SoHo.

DISTANCE: 1.6 miles (2.5km) **ALLOW:** 1.5 hours

START .... **END**

SHEUNG WAN MTR **LI YUEN STREETS EAST AND WEST**
🚇 C9 🚌 Sheung Wan (▷ 45) 🚇 C10 🚌 Central

❶ Start the walk at Sheung Wan MTR station and turn right outside Exit B on Des Voeux Road. Head toward the large Edwardian building of Western Market.

❽ Finally turn right along Stanley Street to head east until Pottinger Street. The walk ends with the narrow market alleys of Pottinger Street and Li Yuen streets East and West (▷ 45).

❷ Head south and turn right at a compass-like piazza on to Wing Lok Street. Tour the traditional Chinese shops selling ginseng, bird's nests and other dried ingredients. Return along Bonham Strand West before heading uphill and turning left on to Hollywood Road (▷ 41).

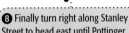

❼ Head downhill across Hollywood Road. Venture down from the escalator corridors to explore the small restaurants of Gage Street and the shops of Lyndhurst Terrace, returning to Cochrane Street below the escalator each time.

❸ After a few bends and the many antiques, curio and jade shops take a left on Lok Ku Road and an immediate right onto the pedestrian route of Upper Lascar Row (Cat Street, ▷ 45).

❻ At the Mid-Levels escalator turn right if in need of the SoHo bars and restaurants, otherwise ascend to the escalator's bridges.

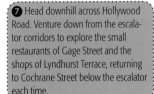

❹ At the end of this souvenir run turn right up the steps of Ladder Street to arrive at Man Mo Temple (▷ 29).

❺ On leaving the temple turn right and continue for some 436 yards (400m) down Hollywood Road.

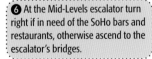

HONG KONG ISLAND WALK

Shopping

CAT STREET MARKET

This shopping complex full of antiques dealers and curio shops is close to the Hollywood Road antiques area.

🔲 B9 ✉ 38 Lok Ku Road, Sheung Wan ☎ 2291 0006 🕐 Mon–Sat 11–7 🚇 Sheung Wan

CHINESE ARTS AND CRAFTS (HK) LTD.

cachk.com

Compared to other Chinese emporia, this one stocks more designer rosewood and lacquer furniture, lamps and carpets. You can find some pretty valuable pieces here. There are three other outlets in Central, Admiralty and TST.

🔲 F10 ✉ 2/F, Causeway Centre, 28 Harbour Road, Wan Chai ☎ 2827 6667 🕐 Daily 10.30–7.30 🚇 Wan Chai

CHOCOLATE RAIN

chocolaterain.com

Chocolate Rain sells hand-made patchwork bags, dolls and jewelry— many pieces have a cutesy chic borrowed from Japanese pop culture. Souvenirs for the fashionably minded.

🔲 C10 ✉ 1/F, PMQ, 35 Aberdeen Street, Central ☎ 2559 0017 🕐 Daily 12–9 🚇 Central

CHOW TAI FOOK

chawtaifook.com

This is just one of a good local jewelry chain that has branches in Causeway Bay, Central and around Mong Kok.

🔲 C10 ✉ G2 Aon China Building, 29 Queen's Road, Central ☎ 2523 7128 🕐 Daily 10–8.30 🚇 Central

ECLECTIC COOL

eclectic-cool.com

A design lover's paradise, Eclectic Cool carries affordable and contemporary home accessories with a vintage vibe. Come here for high-quality souvenirs, snap up a chic mug, candle, stationery, or a set of pretty ceramic bowls.

🔲 E11 ✉ 5 Sun Street, Wan Chai ☎ 2549 6682 🕐 Daily 11–6 🚇 Wan Chai

G.O.D.

god.com.hk

The initials of this Hong Kong boutique stand for "Goods of Desire." It's self-consciously chic, with something to please every taste, from furniture to fashions, music to greetings cards. There are seven more locations dotted around the city.

🔲 C10 ✉ 48 Hollyood Road, Central ☎ 2523 5561 🕐 Mon–Sat 10.30–7, Sun 12.30–7 🚇 Central

ISLAND BEVERLY CENTRE

This treasure trove of youth fashion is well hidden amid the neon splatter in Causeway Bay. Contained within are row after row of small stores and boutiques selling local, Japanese and Korean couture. One for the kids.

🔲 H10 ✉ 1 Great George Street, Causeway Bay ☎ 2890 6823 🕐 Daily noon–11pm 🚇 Causeway Bay

WARRANTIES

Before parting with any money, check whether the warranty is an international one or for Asia. If it is the latter, the price should be lower. Always check a quote with other retailers before making a substantial purchase. When buying software, make sure you know the specs of your hardware and check the minimum memory and speed requirements on the box before you buy. Prices in Hong Kong are comparable to those in the US; Europeans will find some good bargains.

JARDINE'S CRESCENT

Crowds flock to this little lane to bag some imitation fashions at a medley of the area's trendy boutiques and market stalls. Not just good for a daytime visit—the place really comes alive at night.

➕ H10 ✉ Jardine's Crescent, Causeway Bay ⏱ Daily mid-morning to late 🚇 Causeway Bay

KARIN WEBER ANTIQUES

karinwebergallery.com

Here you'll find a mixture of arts and crafts, modern Asian pieces and Chinese country antiques.

➕ C10 ✉ Ground floor, 20 Aberdeen Street, Central ☎ 2544 5004 ⏱ Mon–Sat 11–7, Sun 1–6 🚇 Central

LI YUEN STREET MARKET

Li Yuen Street is one of Hong Kong's oldest markets, where today you'll still find excellent bargains. Come here for clothes, handbags, colorful fabrics and other accessories.

➕ C10 ✉ Off Queen's Road, Central ⏱ Daily 12–late 🚇 Central

MOUNTAIN FOLKCRAFT

mountainfolkcraft.com

Established in 1969, Mountain Folkcraft sells delightful handmade paintings, carvings and *batik* from Southeast Asia.

➕ C10 ✉ 12 Wo On Lane, Central ☎ 2523 2817 ⏱ Mon–Sat 10–6.30 🚇 Central

OI LING ANTIQUES

honeychurch.com

Browse here for antique silverware, utensils and jewelry. The store also offers a range of ornaments and items from around the world.

➕ C10 ✉ 72 Hollywood Road, Central ☎ 2815 9422 ⏱ Mon–Sat 10–7, Sun 1–6.30 🚇 Central

STANLEY MARKET

hk-stanley-market.com

A popular weekend destination, Stanley Market bursts with local artwork, scarves, knick-knacks, fresh fruit vendors, and Chinese accessories all wedged into narrow, labyrinthine lanes.

➕ Off Map F12 ✉ 6 Stanley Market Rd, Stanley ⏱ Daily 10–7 🚇 Stanley

W. W. CHAN & SONS

wwchan.com

Men's suits made by this classy tailor have a life-span of about 20 years and will be altered free of charge at any point during that time. Once they have your measurements, you can order another suit from home.

➕ C10 ✉ Unit B, 8th floor, Entertainment Building, 30 Queen's Road, Central ☎ 2366 9738 ⏱ Mon–Sat 10–7 🚇 Central

WINDSOR HOUSE COMPUTER PLAZA

windsorhouse.hk

A collection of specialist computer shops retailing hardware and software. Stores look more sophisticated than those in Sham Shui Po.

➕ H10 ✉ 10th–12th floors, The In Square, Windsor House, 311 Gloucester Road, Causeway Bay ⏱ Daily 10–10 🚇 Causeway Bay

QTS

Look for the Quality Tourism Services (QTS) logo—a large, gold Q encircling a black Chinese character—in shop windows. This logo means that the shop has been accredited by the Hong Kong Tourism Board (HKTB) and is committed to certain standards. These include providing clear product and price information and also rectifying complaints should anything happen to go wrong.

Entertainment and Nightlife

DJIBOUTII

homekonggroup.com

Slightly off the beaten path, Djiboutii is hidden down a back alley in Wan Chai. It resembles a luxe living room albeit lit up with purple-hued lighting. This is a cool spot for creative cocktails and Mediterranean food.

🔢 E11 ✉ 2 Landale Street, Wan Chai
☎ 9449 0777 🕐 Daily 12–11 🚇 Wan Chai

DRAGON-I

dragon-i.com.hk

Still the most fashionable club in Hong Kong, Dragon-I remains the place to be seen and remains a magnet for the celebrity class. There's a bar, restaurant and a terrace overlooking busy Wyndham Street. Happy hour is 6–9pm.

🔢 C10 ✉ Upper ground floor, The Centrium, 60 Wyndham Street, Central ☎ 3110 1222
🕐 Mon–Sat noon–late 🚇 Central

FRANK'S LIBRARY

mingfathouse.com/restaurants/franks-library

This retro jazz bar isn't the easiest to find, but we'll give you a hint. It's a bar within a bar, hidden inside sister speakeasy Foxglove. Once inside, award-winning mixologist Derek Tsui will spoil you with travel-themed cocktails and barrel-aged concoctions, while live music keeps spirits high.

🔢 D10 ✉ 18 Ice House Street, Central
☎ 2116 8949 🕐 Mon–Thu 6pm–1am, Fri–Sat 6pm–3am 🚇 Central

FRINGE CLUB

hkfringe.com.hk

The Fringe Club is Hong Kong's main venue for non-mainstream performance art, as well as the go-to place for interesting drama workshops. During the Arts Festival, alternative offerings are usually staged.

🔢 C10 ✉ 2 Lower Albert Road, Central
☎ 2521 7251 🕐 Mon–Thu noon–midnight, Fri, Sat noon–3am 🚇 Central

HONG KONG ACADEMY FOR PERFORMING ARTS

hkapa.edu

This arts school next to the Arts Centre has different-size theaters, plus an outdoor venue and provides a full calendar of music, film and varied theater performances.

🔢 E10 ✉ 1 Gloucester Road, Wan Chai
☎ 2584 8500 🚇 Wan Chai

HONG KONG ARTS CENTRE

hkac.org.hk

A diverse line up of drama and musical performances takes place here.

🔢 F10 ✉ 2 Harbour Road, Wan Chai
☎ 2582 0200 🚇 Wan Chai

HONG KONG CITY HALL

cityhall.gov.hk

The stage, auditorium and recital hall host performances by a wide variety of local and visiting artists. It's a popular place to watch Cantonese Opera (see panel below).

🔢 D10 ✉ 5 Edinburgh Place, Central
☎ 2921 2840 🚇 Central

CANTONESE OPERA

Dating back to the 12th century, this is a highly stylized but very energetic art form. The basic story lines follow the local myths. Characters wear startling make-up and gorgeous clothes. Though the Cantonese songs and accompaniment are loud and discordant to Western ears, the acrobatics and swordfights can be stunning. Watch it as a spectacle rather than a story. The audience chats, wanders about and sometimes joins in.

there's a full Spanish menu, too. To add to the atmosphere, wandering musicians serenade you as you eat.
➕ H10 ✉ Ground floor, Florida Mansion, 9–11 Cleveland street, Causeway Bay ☎ 2576 8650 🕐 Mon–Sat noon–1am, Sun noon–3, 6pm–midnight 🚇 Causeway Bay

EL LOCO GRINGO ($$)

casteloconcepts.co

A laid-back Mexican restaurant and bar, great for big groups. For an early week pick-me-up, swing by on Mondays or Tuesdays from 6–11pm for a free flow taco, quesadillas and margaritas deal.
➕ A10 ✉ 49 Bonham Road, Sai Ying Pun ☎ 2858 8833 🕐 Daily 6–10pm 🚇 Sai Ying Pun

FU SING ($$)

Offering an authentic dim sum experience in a modern setting, Fu Sing is known for its baked *char siu bao* with sugar on top. But don't stop there: There are dozens of dim sum options on the menu, including *shumai* (pork and shrimp dumplings), roasted pork, fried tofu, turnip cakes and more.
➕ Off map F11 ✉ 1F, 68 Yee Wo Street, Causeway Bay ☎ 2504 4228 🕐 Daily 11–11 🚇 Causeway Bay

INDONESIAN RESTAURANT 1968 ($$)

ir1968.com

Serving up Indonesian favourites such as *nasi goreng* and *gado gado* since 1968, this stalwart favourite has now moved from its historic home in Causeway Bay to Central but remains a destination for lovers of high quality, well-priced Southeast Asian cuisine.
➕ C10 ✉ 5th Floor, The L Place, 139 Queen's Road, Central ☎ 2577 9981 🕐 Daily noon–midnight 🚇 Central

JIMMY'S KITCHEN ($$)

jimmys.com

Jimmy's has been serving food to the people of Hong Kong since the 1920s, which says a lot in this ever-evolving city. Staying true to its roots, the menu can be relied on for its signature goulash, borscht and stroganoff. The interiors provide a comfortable dining atmosphere with consistent and reliable service.
➕ C10 ✉ South China Building, 1 Wyndham Street, Central ☎ 2526 5293 🕐 Daily 12–3, 6–11 🚇 Central

JUMBO KINGDOM ($$$)

jumbo.com

Decorated with dragon sculptures and gold motifs, this opulent boat restaurant is a tourist attraction in itself. But don't miss the excellent Chinese cuisine served on board. It's an unforgettable night out that begins with a free ferry ride in a small *sampan* that takes you across the harbor.
➕ Off map ✉ Jumbo Kingdom, Shan Wan Pier Drive, Aberdeen ☎ 2553 9111 🕐 Daily 11am–11.30pm 🚌 7, 70 from Central Bus Terminal

LOBSTER BAR AND GRILL ($$$)

shangri-la.com

In Hong Kong's Shangri-La Hotel, the swanky yet relaxed Lobster Bar and Grill is known for its live music, superlative service and excellent bar atmosphere. The restaurant serves an innovative modern European menu—try the bluefin tuna with asparagus and egg-plant (aubergine) salad—while the bar is a favorite go to for cocktail and wine lovers.
➕ E11 ✉ 6th Floor, Island Shangri-La, Pacific Place, Supreme Court Road, Central ☎ 2820 8560 🕐 Daily 12–3; 6.30–10 🚇 Central

MAN WAH RESTAURANT ($$$)

mandarinoriental.com

Unlike most Chinese restaurants, the Man Wah is dimly lit, intimate and elegant, as you would expect in Hong Kong's Mandarin Hotel. The food is excellent and well worth the money.

🔳 D10 ✉ 25th Floor, Mandarin Oriental Hotel, 5 Connaught Road, Central ☎ 2825 4003 🕐 Daily 7am–11am, Mon–Fri 12–3, 6.30–11 🚇 Central

MAXIM'S PALACE ($$)

maxims.com.hk

One of the few places where you can enjoy dim sum from hand-pushed trolleys, this is a vast dim sum institution that's very popular for family brunch on Sundays. Prices here are reasonable and there are great harbor views, but be sure to get there early to avoid a long line.

🔳 D10 ✉ 3rd Floor, City Hall, 5–7 Edinburgh Place, Central ☎ 2521 1303 🕐 Mon–Sat 11–3, 5.30–11, Sun 9–3, 5.30–11 🚇 Central

THE PAWN ($$)

thepawn.com

This 19th-century pawn shop opened as a restaurant-bar some 10 years ago and underwent a complete overhaul in 2014 when acclaimed British chef, Tom Aikens, joined the team. It's modern British cuisine in the main room, and there's also a lounge bar and rooftop garden to enjoy.

🔳 F11 ✉ 62 Johnston Road, Wan Chai ☎ 2866 3444 🕐 Daily noon–midnight 🚇 Wan Chai

PEAK CAFÉ BAR ($)

cafedecogroup.com

This bar and café cannot be missed thanks to its perch along the Mid-Levels Escalator. Inside is an interesting mixture of old-world Chinese decor, dramatic Gothic stonework and lighting from sparkling chandeliers.

🔳 C10 ✉ 9–13 Shelley Street, Central ☎ 2140 6877 🕐 Mon–Fri 11am–2am, Sat 9am–2am, Sun 9am–midnight 🚇 Central

TOKIO JOE ($$)

lkfe.com

A trendy spot in Lan Kwai Fong, Tokio Joe serves good sushi and sashimi, as well as filled rolls and hot dishes. The same company has other Japanese establishments in the area, including Kyoto Joel.

🔳 C10 ✉ 16 Lan Kwai Fong, Central ☎ 2525 1889 🕐 Mon–Sat 12–2.30, 6.30–11, Sun 6.30–11 🚇 Central

YUNG KEE RESTAURANT ($$)

yungkee.com

This long-standing favorite among local people is known as *the* place to eat Cantonese cuisine in the area. Yung Kee has a list of prestigious awards to support its reputation. The restaurant is easy to find, thanks to its location in the heart of Central. Look for the large, glamorous shop front and valet parking services.

🔳 C10 ✉ 32–40 Wellington Street, Central ☎ 2522 1624 🕐 11–11 🚇 Central

---

CHOPSTICKS

● Hold one chopstick between your thumb joint and the tip of your third finger.

● Hold the other chopstick between the tip of your thumb and the tips of your first and second fingers.

● Keep the first chopstick rigid. Move the second one up and down to grab food.

● Put food from the serving dish on top of rice, hold the bowl close to your mouth and push the food in with your chopsticks.

Kowloon

Densely populated Kowloon is where Hong Kong's gritty daily life happens. There are shops everywhere, and if you have a hankering for real Chinese food, this is where to find it.

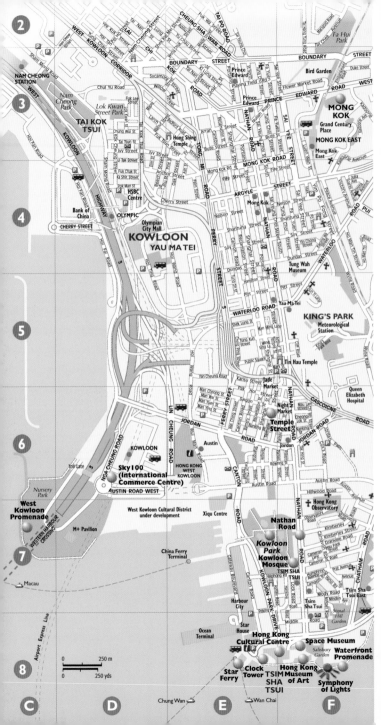

Kowloon

Old Kai Tak Airport

KOWLOON CITY

Theatre

BOUNDARY STREET
EDWARD ROAD WEST
PRINCE

Flint Road
Lincoln Road

ARGYLE STREET

MA TAU WAI

KAI TAK TUNNEL
Kai Tak Cruise Terminal

SUNG WONG TOI ROAD

MA TAU KOK

Tweed Road
Dunbar Road
Perth Street

ARGYLE STREET

Farm Road

Kowloon City Ferry Pier

MARGARET
FAT KWONG
CHING ROAD

HO MAN TIN

MA TAU WAI ROAD

CITY ROAD

TO KWA WAN

Ko-Shan Theatre Park

Ko-Shan Theatre

Hoi Sham Park

PRINCESS

FAT KWONG STREET

KOWLOON EAST

MA TAU WAI ROAD

Bailey Street

TO KWA WAN

Kowloon Bay

Hok Yuen Street
Hok Yuen St East
Tsing Chau Street
Lee Kung Street
Man Yue Street

SUNG ON ST

Kun Yam Temple

Hutchison Park

HUNG HOM

Tai Wan Shan Park

GILLIES AVENUE

Winslow Street

HUNG HOM ROAD

Dyer Avenue

Whampoa

Hong Kong Polytechnic University

Hong Kong Museum of History

Science Museum

SALISBURY

HUNG HOM STATION

Hong Kong Coliseum

HUNG HOM BYPASS

Hung Hom Ferry Pier

North Point

TSIM SHA TSUI EAST

CROSS HARBOUR TUNNEL

Victoria Harbour

G   H   J

Hong Kong Museum of Art

Modern art on display at the Hong Kong Museum of Art (right)

THE BASICS

lcsd/gov.hk/CE/
Museum/Arts

✚ F8

✉ 10 Salisbury Road
(next door to Hong Kong
Cultural Centre)

☎ 2721 0116

🕐 Mon–Wed, Fri 10–6,
Sat–Sun 10–7

🍴 Museum café

🚇 Tsim Sha Tsui

🚌 Tsim Sha Tsui bus
station

⛴ Star Ferry from Wan
Chai and Central to Tsim
Sha Tsui

♿ Excellent

✋ Inexpensive; free Wed

❓ Museum bookshop

HIGHLIGHTS

● Han-dynasty pottery
watchtower
● Tang-dynasty tomb
guardians
● Translucent rhino-horn
cups
● Painting of Wyndham
Street
● Model of Guangzhou

A beautifully laid-out series of galleries contains displays of traditional and modern Chinese calligraphy and paintings, ancient artifacts and a collection of jade, ivory and pottery.

Chinese antiquities The museum has several galleries, many of which contain Chinese antiquities, local artists' works and pictures of historical note as well as artistic worth. The thousands of exhibits in the Chinese antiquities section range from rhino-horn cups to burial goods and lavish tomb adornments; of special interest are two large Tang dynasty (AD618–906) tomb guardians in the form of mythical beasts. The jade and ivory carvings in the decorative arts gallery are lovely.

Art galleries The best gallery is the one containing old pictures and prints of Hong Kong. It is hard to believe that the sandy beaches and jungle-filled hills could have become such a different kind of jungle in such a short stretch of time. It is a revelation of just how far the colony has come since the early 19th century.

Modern art The works in the contemporary art gallery are divided into decades, and it is interesting to see the development of local art since the 1950s. There is also a collection of calligraphy and Chinese paintings, and a special gallery for international exhibitions. Between galleries, armchairs facing the vast corridor windows allow views of the waterfront.

Hong Kong Museum of History

Easy to navigate and uber informative, this gem of a museum is a good place to spend an hour or two, especially as the curators frequently introduce new shows and exhibits.

Before the handover When the administrative body of HK SAR built this $390 million history museum, you had to wonder at how they might choose to explain the territory's history. But instead of brushing over inconvenient truths, the museum is an excellent portrayal of the area from prehistory to the 1997 handover. The displays are interactive, with sounds and smells, and there are even walk-through exhibits like a Hakka family dwelling or an early tram.

Exhibits The natural history section documents most of the wildlife that has ever roamed these parts, while the archaeology area, covering about 6,000 years of history, tells the story of the island's earliest settlers. Most of the objects uncovered at Lei Cheng Uk (▷ 67) are here, too. There's an ethnography section explaining where all Hong Kongers originated from. The real interest of the museum, though, is its account of more modern history. There are exhibits on the Japanese occupation (laid out as an air-raid shelter), Hong Kong's development and even a bit about what has happened since it became one of China's SARs. Stamps, old documents and a huge photographic collection make a visit to this fascinating museum anything but dull.

THE BASICS

history.museum

✚ F7/G7

✉ 100 Chatham Road South, Tsim Sha Tsui

☎ 2724 9042

🕐 Mon, Wed–Fri 10–6, Sat–Sun 10–7

🍴 Café in museum

🚇 Tsim Sha Tsui East

🚌 5, 5C, 8 from Star Ferry

♿ Excellent

✋ Inexpensive (free Wed)

HIGHLIGHTS

● The photographic collection
● Reconstructions of a tea shop, grocer's, barber's and cinema from the 1960s
● The re-created street from the early years of the last century with tram, boat, herbalists and more
● Reconstruction of the Bogue forts used in the Opium Wars

Kowloon Walled City Park

This park stands on the site of the former Walled City

THE BASICS

lcsd.gov.hk/en/parks/kwcp/index.html

➕ H2

✉ Junction of Tung Tau Tsuen and Tung Tsing roads, Kowloon

🕐 Daily 6.30am–11pm

🚌 Bus 101 from Central; Lok Fu Exit B then take a taxi to Tung Tau Tsuen Road

♿ Good

🎟 Free

HIGHLIGHTS

● Pretty, quiet space in the middle of Kowloon
● Turtle and goldfish ponds
● Artistic topiary
● Renovated administrative building

TIPS

● This is a great place to enjoy a picnic.
● If you have your own chess pieces, you can have a game on the park's large Chinese chessboards.

Once the most notorious, lawless and poverty-stricken place in Hong Kong, Kowloon Walled City is now a manicured park, filled with pavilions, topiary and shady walks. Even the shrubs have been cut and shaped into animal figures.

From ruin to park In 1898, when Britain leased the New Territories from China, Kowloon Walled City was a Chinese garrison and was never included in any agreement. The two countries bickered over its jurisdiction for almost 100 years while the area became ever more ramshackle, with blocks of tenements raised without any kind of planning; nonexistent sanitation led to frequent outbreaks of disease. During World War II the Japanese knocked the walls down to extend the old Kai Tak airport and thousands of illegal immigrants from China found a post-war refuge there. The two governments finally reached a settlement in 1987. The 30,000 inhabitants were rehoused and the buildings were flattened. After archaeologists rummaged around, finally a park was built in the ruins. The park is complete with pagodas, a Chinese zodiac garden, a mountain view pavilion and a hilltop pavilion.

Historic survivor One of the original buildings of the fort, the Yamen, dating back to the 19th century, has been restored and holds a display of photos and items concerning the history of the Walled City, including the stone plaques that marked the south gate of the Walled City.

Interactive exhibits at the Science Museum, including Hong Kong's first airliner

Science Museum

The Science Museum is one of Hong Kong's most popular attractions. In such a modern city, some of the 500 major exhibits feel a bit old-fashioned these days, but children will still love them.

Still popular Exhibitions include objects from the past as well as explaining how everyday items function, and some focus on the science and technology particularly relevant to Hong Kong. The museum's 18 galleries across four floors contain thousands of exhibits, most of them interactive, especially in the children's areas. Topics cover all aspects of science but it's the sheer scale of some of the exhibits that makes the science interesting. In one gallery, a DC3 plane hangs from the ceiling, while a kinetic energy machine rises through all four floors of the museum and sends hundreds of balls pulsing around a metallic labyrinth.

For children The museum is definitely a child-oriented place and on weekdays it's packed with school children Two exhibits are in huge demand here—a car linked up to a video screen where children can try to drive around the computer-simulated road in front of them and a similar setup with a whole light aircraft. Exhibits cover the entire spectrum of science-related subjects, from electricity and magnetism to a breakdown of what you eat. There are robot arms to operate, buttons to push and a machine that calculates the minute-by-minute increase in the world's population.

THE BASICS

hk.science.museum

F7/G7

2 Science Museum Road, Tsim Sha Tsui East

2732 3232

Mon–Wed, Fri 10–7, Sat–Sun 10–9

Café

Tsim Sha Tsui East

5, 5C, 8 from Star Ferry

Good

Moderate (free Wed)

HIGHLIGHTS

● Simulated interactive rides
● Giant energy tower
● Irresistible knobs to press
● Watching the school children swarm onto the exhibits

TIPS

● School parties usually arrive mid-afternoon.
● Sunday is a very popular day for families.
● The Hong Kong Museum of History is close by if you want to make a day of it.

Space Museum

HIGHLIGHTS

- IMAX shows
- Mercury space capsule
- Hall of Space Science
- Solar telescope
- Planetarium show
- Hall of Astronomy

TIPS

- Some of the interactive exhibits have height and weight restrictions.
- If there is a typhoon or a black rainstorm warning, the museum will close.

This museum, which has one of the world's most advanced planetariums, is fascinating for kids, with plenty of hands-on exhibits, a *Mercury* space capsule and daily Space Theatre shows.

Layout and IMAX The museum's distinctive oval, pink facade, built in 1980 by the Architectural Services Department, is in itself stunning. Inside are three exhibitions: the Hall of Astronomy, the Hall of Space Science and, the most popular, the Stanley Ho Space Theatre with its 75ft (23m) screen. If you have time for an IMAX film, seize the chance here. You'll sit back in tilted seats and gaze up at a screen that covers most of the ceiling and front wall. The shows here alternate between star shows using a star projector and IMAX shows from around

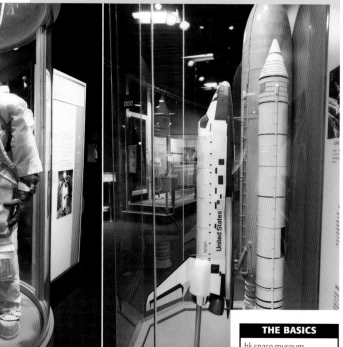

Clockwise from left: A solar system display in the Hall of Astonomy; a replica of a protective suit used by Apollo astronauts on the moon landing; the model of Space Shuttle Columbia in the Hall of Space Science

the world. The vast size of the screen allows an almost 360-degree panorama.

Exhibition halls The Hall of Space Science includes bits of moon rock, the actual *Mercury* space capsule piloted by Scott Carpenter in 1962, and lots of information about China's current space program. In the Hall of Astronomy there is a solar telescope where you can look directly at the sun. Did you know that it was ancient Chinese astronomers who were the first to spot Halley's Comet and the first to chart the movements of the stars? The interactive simulators include a gyroscope and models allowing you to launch spaceships, land a craft on the moon, take a moon walk or go hang gliding. Great lectures are available for those with an interest in space.

THE BASICS

hk.space.museum

F8

10 Salisbury Road (next to Hong Kong Cultural Centre), Tsim Sha Tsui

2721 0226

Sat–Sun 10–9, Mon, Wed–Fri 1–9

Tsim Sha Tsui

Tsim Sha Tsui bus station

Star Ferry from Central and Wan Chai to Tsim Sha Tsui

Excellent

Inexpensive; free Wed

Children under 3 are not allowed in the IMAX

Star Ferry

- Shops in Tsim Sha Tsui ferry terminal
- Vista to east and west along shipping lane
- Panoramic views of Hong Kong Island
- Hong Kong Maritime Museum
- Views of Peak and Mid Levels

The Star Ferry journey has to be one of the world's most spectacular sea crossings. You get a panoramic view of the harbor as you tack around dredgers, launches and all the other vessels.

Looking back The journey time on this ferry, which has been operating between Kowloon and Hong Kong Island since 1898, is less than 10 minutes on a good day, but the views of the city-scape are excellent—and all for HK$2.70 weekdays, $3.70 weekends. The ferry terminal on the Tsim Sha Tsui side sits beside the Hong Kong Cultural Centre (1989), with its window-less, tiled surface (▷ 67). As the ferry sets off to Hong Kong Island, you can see the pink-and-black striped outlines of the Hong Kong Museum of Art (▷ 54).

Riding the Star Ferry across Victoria Harbour is something every visitor to Hong Kong should experience

Looking ahead On the island itself, the architecture of the reclaimed shoreline pierces the sky. The most eye-catching section begins with the Convention and Exhibition Centre, which juts out beside the Wan Chai Pier and is framed by Central Plaza. Next door is the Central Government Complex and the Prince of Wales Building, home to the Chinese People's Liberation Army. To the right, I.M. Pei's Bank of China Tower is clearly visible beside the soaring monolith of the Cheung Tak Centre. Finally, behind Central's Star Ferry Pier is the IFC complex, with Two IFC, at 1,362ft (415m), the tallest building on Hong Kong Island. The Hong Kong Maritime Museum (open daily) occupies three floors within Central Ferry Pier 8 and is well worth a visit. In addition, the Star Ferry runs organized tours around the harbor.

THE BASICS

starferry.com.hk

🚇 E8

✉ Salisbury Road, Tsim Sha Tsui (Kowloon); Man Yui Street, Central (Hong Kong Island); Sea Front Road, Wan Chai (Hong Kong Island)

☎ Hotline: 2367 7065

🕐 Daily 6.30am–11.30pm. Office: 8.30am–6.30pm

🍴 Cafés, bakeries at Central ferry terminal gate

Ⓜ Tsim Sha Tsui (Kowloon); Central, Wan Chai (Hong Kong Island)

♿ Lower decks more accessible

💷 Inexpensive

Symphony of Lights

HIGHLIGHTS

● Harbor trip
● The breezy Tsim Sha Tsui promenade
● Occasional pyrotechnic additions to the show
● The view beyond the harborfront to the Peak

TIPS

● Several tour companies offer 1.5-hour, drinks-included tours of the harbor.
● Star Ferries' tour (no drinks) is the least expensive at HK$170 for 1 hour.

Victoria Harbour has to be one of the most amazing sights of a trip to Hong Kong. Each evening a stunning sound-and-light show takes place creating a vibrant frenzy along the waterfront.

Dazzling display Impressive though it has always been, Victoria Harbour is even more striking since the introduction of a Symphony of Lights. It is a stirring experience to watch this 10-minute performance on Hong Kong Island and Kowloon. Every day at 8pm, the exteriors of 40 of the city's major buildings glow with vivid colors, with the use of a wide range of LED lights to draw the eye along the waterfront. Best viewed from Tsim Sha Tsui, the spectacle sees one building after another light up, high-lighting its outline or changing its appearance

Spectacular views of the skyscrapers on Hong Kong Island are lit up by the dazzling Symphony of Lights

altogether. With the addition of several buildings Kowloon-side, the lights and lasers reach right across the harbor, turning the whole area into a dazzling display. A narration and music are broadcast each night along the Avenue of Stars, while onlookers from Tsim Sha Tsui and Golden Bauhinia Square in Wan Chai can tune into the narration by radio (English channel available on 103.4FM). On certain special occasions, the light display is complemented by rooftop pyrotechnic displays on some buildings. You can also take one of the harbor cruises and listen to the narration and music piped aboard.

Take an evening stroll The striking display is recognized by the *Guinness Book of Records* as the largest permanent sound-and-light show in the world.

THE BASICS

tourism.gov.hk/symphony

➕ F8

🕐 8pm–8.18pm

🚇 Tsim Sha Tsui, Wan Chai

♿ Good

✋ Free

Temple Street

TOP 25

Grab a bargain at Temple Street Night Market

THE BASICS

🚇 E6

✉ Temple Street, Kansu Street, Reclamation Street, Kowloon

🕐 Jade market: 10–5. Temple Street market: 4pm–midnight. Vegetable market: early morning and early evening

🍴 Seafood restaurants and hawker area on Temple Street

🚇 Jordan

♿ Good

🖐 Free

HIGHLIGHTS

● Fresh fish for sale
● Fortune-tellers
● Chinese medicine shops
● Shops selling traditional Chinese wedding clothes
● Jade market
● Yau Ma Tei Typhoon Shelter, to the west
● Racks of T-shirts
● Exotic vegetables in vegetable market

At about 4pm each afternoon, stands appear on either side of this street and are hung with T-shirts, lingerie, jeans and other goodies. Earlier in the day, nearby stalls do a brisk trade in jade.

After dark The market is full of bargains—silk shirts, leather items, jeans, gadgets, tea ware and T-shirts—and local bargain hunters. After about 2pm the street is closed to traffic as the stalls are set up. Restaurants line the street to the north and south of the main market throng, and pull plastic tables and chairs onto the street after dark. This is one of a few places where it's still possible to eat under the stars in downtown Hong Kong.

Jade for sale Close by, near the junction of Battery and Kansu streets, under an overpass, is the jade market. Here, hundreds of stands sell all kinds of jade, which comes in many shades besides green––from white through to purple. Prices range from inexpensive to a king's ransom.

Still more In adjoining streets are vegetable and fruit sellers, shops selling fabrics and traditional red-embroidered Chinese wedding ensembles and many Chinese medicine shops. You may even catch a Cantonese opera performance, near the Tin Hau Temple to the north of the street. As you walk through the market, look for people playing the age-old game of mahjong in the backs of shops or in corners.

Waterfront Promenade

The views of Hong Kong Island and the harbor are outstanding all along the length of this promenade on the Kowloon waterfront.

Avenue of Stars Even before the creation of the Avenue of Stars, the Waterfront Promenade was an excellent place for an evening's stroll, close to the chaos of Nathan Road but serene, and, above all, relatively unpopulated, especially toward its eastern end popular with old fishermen and canoodling lovers. Nowadays the 0.25-mile (400m) Avenue of Stars (recently renovated), a tribute to the 100 years or so of movie making in Hong Kong, draws the crowds. Represented here are some of the people responsible for the huge success of the industry. At least 20 celebrities have sunk their handprints into the cement blocks set into the ground.

Statues There are also statues of the stars and a giant model of the statuette given out at the Hong Kong Awards ceremony each year. All the big names are here, plus some you may never have heard of. Accompanying the plaques is a series of pillars that tell the history of film making. The lifelike statue of Bruce Lee was built from funds donated by his fans.

Weekends On weekends you will see engaged couples posing for photos here, with the skyline of Hong Kong Island behind them. On Saturday evenings there are free music performances.

THE BASICS

- ✚ F8
- ✉ Salisbury Road
- 🍴 Nearby
- 🚇 Tsim Sha Tsui
- ♿ Excellent
- 💲 Free

HIGHLIGHTS

- ● Statue of Bruce Lee
- ● The view of the harbor
- ● Watching people posing by the statues
- ● The quieter eastern end

TIPS

- ● The evening is the best time to visit.
- ● Find a spot on the Avenue of Stars to watch the Symphony of Lights.

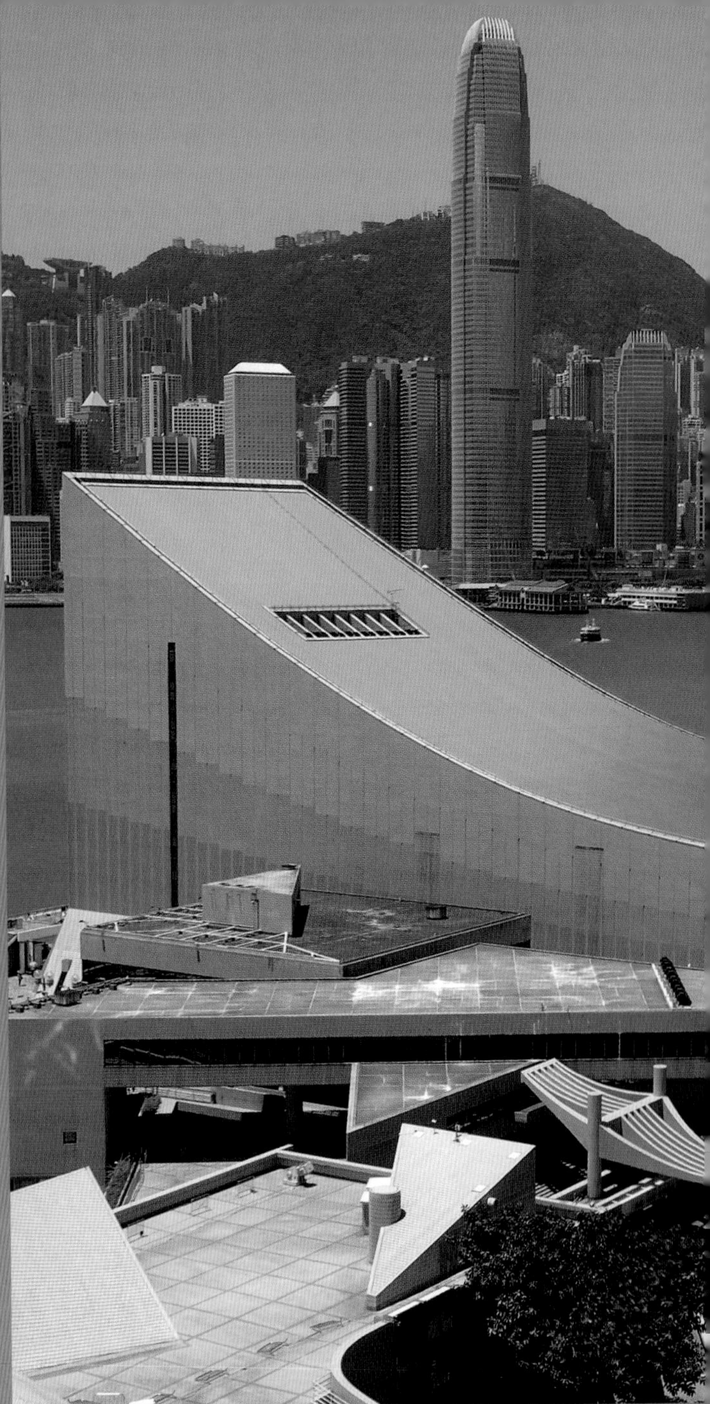

More to See

CLOCK TOWER

amo.gov.hk/en/monuments_43.php
The 148ft (45m) clock tower is all
that remains of the Kowloon–
Canton Railway Station—once the
final stop of a rail network that
stretched all the way to Europe.
🚻 E8 ✉ Salisbury Road 🍴 Nearby
🚇 Tsim Sha Tsui ♿ Excellent

HONG KONG CULTURAL CENTRE

hkculturalcentre.gov.hk
Designed by the government's
architectural services department in
1989, this is one of Hong Kong's
most controversial buildings. It has
a huge sloping roof and is uniformly
pink. The building is also window-
less—rather odd as it would have
one of the most stunning views in
the world. Inside, it is ultramodern,
especially the sparse auditoria with
their apparently unsupported
balconies. At the rear is a waterfront walkway.
🚻 E/F8 ✉ Salisbury Road, Tsim Sha Tsui
☎ 3185 1612 🚇 Tsim Sha Tsui ✋ Free

KOWLOON MOSQUE

kowloonmosque.com
Built on the site of an earlier
19th-century one, this is the
largest mosque in Hong Kong.
🚻 F7 ✉ Corner of Nathan and Haiphong
roads ☎ 2724 0095 to arrange a visit
🕐 Closed to general public 🍴 Nearby
🚇 Tsim Sha Tsui

KOWLOON PARK

lcsd.gov.hk/parks/kp/indexc.html
Kowloon Park is full of fun things to
do. There's an open-air and an
indoor swimming pool, an aviary, a
Chinese garden and much more. In
the morning you can watch people
practising t'ai chi.
🚻 E7 ✉ Nathan Road 🕐 Daily 5am–
midnight 🍴 Cafés and restaurants in Nathan
Road 🚇 Tsim Sha Tsui ♿ Poor ✋ Free

LEI CHENG UK TOMB MUSEUM

lcsd.gov.hk/ce/Museum/History/en/lcuht.php
Although built over an ancient Han
dynasty tomb, this little museum is
now surrounded by glossy high-rise
apartments, creating a continuity

Hong Kong Cultural Centre (left), Kowloon Mosque (above)

between the living and the deceased, which spans more than 2,000 years.

🔲 Off map at D1 ⊠ 41 Tonkin Street, Sham Shui Po ☎ 2386 2863 🕑 Mon–Wed, Fri and Sat 10–6. Closed 25–26 Dec and first 3 days of Chinese New Year 🚇 Cheung Sha Wan 🚌 2 from Star Ferry to Po On Road 🚻 Good access to museum displays but not to tomb 🖐 Free

MONG KOK

Mong Kok's crowded streets, tenements and markets are well worth experiencing. The Bird Garden, the Ladies' Market, the Flower Market and the Goldfish Market are all very popular.

🔲 F3 🚇 Mong Kok MTR, KCR 🚻 Poor

NATHAN ROAD

Named after Sir Matthew Nathan, a governor of Hong Kong in the early 20th century, the road is 3.2 miles (5km) long. The southern stretch is known as the "Golden Mile," reflecting local real estate prices.

🔲 F7 🍴 Many 🚇 Tsim Sha Tsui 🚻 Poor

SKY100

sky100.com.hk

On the 100th floor of the ICC (International Commerce Centre) is the Sky100 observation deck which promises staggering 360-degree views of the city. Rising to 1,588ft (484m), the ICC is Hong Kong's tallest building.

🔲 D6 🚇 100th Floor, ICC, 1 Austin Road West, Kowloon ☎ 2613 3888 🕑 Daily 10–9 🚇 Kowloon 🖐 Moderate 🚻 Good

WEST KOWLOON PROMENADE

westkowloon.hk

This sculpted parkland and woodland is a great place to explore. Use an Octopus card (▷ 119) to hire a SmartBike, from one of two hire points, to get around. Here, you'll also find the M+ museum of visual culture and the Xiqu Centre for Cantonese opera.

🔲 D7 ⊠ West Kowloon Cultural District ☎ SmartBike: 6182 3481 🕑 Park Daily 6am–11pm; SmartBike hire Mon–Fri 2–9, Sat–Sun 10–7 🚇 Kowloon 🖐 Park free; SmartBike moderate 🚻 Good

Bustling Nathan Road

Sky100

Symphony of Lights and a Pub Crawl

An evening stroll along the waterfront of TST followed by some of the best places to eat and drink in Kowloon. Start the walk at 8pm.

DISTANCE: 1 mile (1.5km) **ALLOW:** 45 minutes, plus drinking time

START ....

TSIM SHA TSUI STAR FERRY TERMINAL
🚏 E8 ⛴ Star Ferry

1 Head toward the Clock Tower (▷ 67), which is the best place to watch the Symphony of Lights (▷ 62) at 8pm. Follow the waterfront past the Hong Kong Cultural Centre (▷ 67) and the Hong Kong Museum of Art (▷ 54).

2 Head down the Avenue of Stars promenade (▷ 65). Take in the amazing views across the waterfront.

3 Double back toward the Space Museum (▷ 58–59) on Salisbury Road. Cross Salisbury Road via the underpass to arrive at the southern end of Nathan Road. Head north.

4 At the Chungking Mansions, turn left down Peking Road to the One Peking Road building. Head up to the top floor for a cocktail at Aqua Spirit (▷ 72).

.... **END**

HILLWOOD ROAD
🚏 F6 🚇 Jordan

8 The bars here have a more local feel and some strange names.

7 Head for the district of SoHo: turn right onto Observatory Road, left onto Kimberly, stay on the left onto Austin Avenue and keep an eye peeled for the stairs on the left that lead up to Hillwood Road.

6 Wander north through the park, then bear right to rejoin Nathan Road around the Kimberley Road junction. Take the next left up Knutsford Steps into Knutsford Terrace. Here you should enjoy a well-earned rest in one of the lively bars. This street also has a number of great restaurants to consider.

5 Returning down Peking Road, turn left at Hankow Road to reach Maphong Road and the southern entrance to Kowloon Park.

Shopping

BROADWAY

broadwaylifestyle.com

This is one of the biggest branches of a Hong Kong-wide electronics and electrical chain that sells everything from washing machines to electric razors. Most major brands are available at marked-down prices, which are more or less fixed, although you might get a free gift thrown in. You can get a good idea here of a sensible local price, and then move on to serious haggling in some smaller, pushier place if that's what you really want to do.

E4 Ground–3rd Floor, 79 Argyle Street, Mong Kok 2381 9819 Daily 11–10 Mong Kok

ELISSA COHEN JEWELLERY

elissacohen.com

This place is a bit more exciting than the standard jewelry shop chains. Lots of individually designed pieces but higher prices to match.

F7 209 Hankow Centre, 5–15 Hankow Road 2312 0811 Mon–Fri 9–5.30, Sat 9–1 Tsim Sha Tsui

FESTIVAL WALK

festivalwalk.com.hk

One of Hong Kong's most attractive malls, Festival Walk is a weekend destination in itself for many locals, with its own cinema and ice-rink, in addition to the expected boutiques. It's right beside the Kowloon Tong metro interchange.

F1 80–88 Tat Chee Avenue, Kowloon Tong 2844 2222 11–10 Kowloon Tong

GRANVILLE ROAD

Small boutiques selling mid-priced youth labels line this trendy street in Tsim Sha Tsui. There are many more within the Rise Shopping Arcade and nearby Beverly Shopping Centre on Chatham Road South. Inspiration, and custom, is provided by the nearby Hong Kong Polytechnic University which boasts one of Asia's top design schools.

F7/G7 Granville Road Daily 10–9 Tsim Sha Tsui

HARBOUR CITY

harbourcity.com.hk

Compromising five interlinking malls, this goliath building has branches of upmarket international and local boutiques such as Givenchy and Swank, as well as an excellent Marks and Spencer and local chain stores such as G2000.

E8 3-27 Canton Road, Tsim Sha Tsui, Kowloon 2118 8666 Daily 10–10 Tsim Sha Tsui

JUST GOLD

justgold.cc

Popular Hong Kong chain of reasonably priced jewelry stores. Fixed prices and a bit on the kitsch side but stress-free.

F7 Shop 1-33D, 1/F, SOGO, 20 Nathan Road, Tsim Sha Tsui 3911 1949 Daily 10–10 Tsim Sha Tsui

LADIES' MARKET

The long stretch of Tung Choi Street, between Argyle Street and Dundas Street, is home to the daily Ladies' Market, so called for the enormous amount of female fashion. There are also home furnishings, CDs, accessories and trinkets available. It's cramped and claustrophobic, and haggling is essential.

E3 Tung Choi Street Daily 2–10.30 Mong Kok

MONG KOK COMPUTER CENTRE

mongkokcc.com

This small shopping block is crammed with tiny shops that spill out into the

teeming corridors. The vendors are knowledgeable and catalogs of prices are on display. Hardware is mostly Asian-made: computers, monitors, printers and add-on boards. Warranties are usually only for Asia, but prices are competitive.

🔹 E4 ✉ 8–8a Nelson Street, Mong Kok 🕐 Daily 10–10 🚇 Mong Kok

ORIENTAL ARTS JEWELRY

You'll find a wide selection of jade at this sophisticated shop within the Peninsula Hotel's upscale arcade. Also, for those who like to make their own jewelry, there is a large range of beads and stones available to purchase loose.

🔹 F8 ✉ Mezzanine, Peninsula Hotel Shopping Arcade, Salisbury Road, Tsim Sha Tsui 🕐 2369 0820 🕐 Daily 10–8 🚇 Tsim Sha Tsui

RISE COMMERCIAL BUILDING

This "micro mall" is filled with small boutiques carrying the handiwork of local designers, as well as affordable imports from Japan and Korea.

🔹 F7 ✉ 5–11 Granville Circuit, Tsim Sha Tsui 🕐 Various 🕐 Daily 1–11pm 🚇 Tsim Sha Tsui

SAM'S TAILOR

samstailor.com

A Hong Kong institution, Sam's Tailor counts the Duke of Kent and Rod Stewart among its clientele. Sam's Tailor is most famous for its 24-hour suits.

🔹 F7 ✉ Burlington Arcade K&L, 90–94C Nathan Road, Tsim Sha Tsui 🕐 2367 9423 🕐 Mon–Sat 10–7 🚇 Tsim Sha Tsui

STOREROOMS

storerooms.hk

Artsy and airy, this cool indie shop showcases a collection of lifestyle and fashion accessories ranging from trendy sunnies to vintage bags, handmade shoes, reusable water bottles and colorful watches from international brands such as Novesta, Andrea Gallardo and Life & Thread.

🔹 F4 ✉ Shop 44, 3/F, Sai Yeung Choi Street South, Mong Kok 🕐 2426 6789 🕐 Daily 2–9pm 🚇 Mong Kok

TSE SUI LUEN JEWELLERY

tslj.com

Branches of this store sell fairly traditional jewelry designs and watches. Stores in Queen's Road, Central, Causeway Bay and Nathan Road.

🔹 F7 ✉ Shop A&B, Ground Floor, 190 Nathan Road, Tsim Sha Tsui 🕐 2926 3210 🕐 Daily 10am–10.30pm 🚇 Jordan

YUE HWA CHINESE PRODUCTS EMPORIUM

yuehwa.com

A more everyday shop than other, more centrally located Chinese emporia, Yue Hwa sells inexpensive but beautiful dinner services, embroideries, pricey and inexpensive jewelry, workaday silk items and Chinese herbal medicines.

🔹 F6 ✉ 301 Nathan Road, Kowloon 🕐 3511 2222 🕐 Daily 10–10 🚇 Jordan

---

MADE TO MEASURE

Perhaps the most distinctive aspect of men's fashion in Hong Kong is the sheer number and quality of tailors and the nearly unbeatable prices. If you intend to have a suit made in Hong Kong, you should make finding a tailor that you like a priority. The more time and fittings the tailor has, the better the suit will be: A good tailor can make a suit in just 24 hours, but a few days will yield a better, less expensive suit. Some tailors offer a mail-order service.

Entertainment and Nightlife

ALL NIGHT LONG

No website

A live music bar, All Night Long is hidden away in the popular little haven of good places to come for a drink off Knutsford Terrace.

➕ F6 ✉ 9 Knutsford Terrace ☎ 2367 9487
🕐 Sun–Thu 4pm–5am, Fri–Sat 4pm–6am
🚇 Tsim Sha Tsui

AQUA SPIRIT

aqua.com.hk

This is a breathtaking cocktail lounge above two of Kowloon's trendiest restaurants. The views toward Hong Kong Island are some of the best you'll see. This is an essential stop for out-of-towners.

➕ F7 ✉ 30F, 1 Peking Road, Tsim Sha Tsui, Kowloon ☎ 3427 2288 🕐 Daily 4pm–2am
🚇 Tsim Sha Tsui

CASTRO'S

Hidden up an unmarked stairwell in Tsim Sha Tsui, Castro's is one of Hong Kong's best low-key bars. The Cuban-inspired surrounds feature all kinds of memorabilia, plus a menu full of tropical cocktails and draft beers.

➕ E8 ✉ 16 Ashley Road, Tsim Sha Tsui
☎ 2957 8041 🕐 Daily noon–2am 🚇 Tsim Sha Tsui

DELANEY'S KOWLOON

delaneys.com.hk

The design inside Delaney's evokes the look and ambience of a Victorian Irish store and pub. There's live traditional music, Irish food—and Guinness on draft. You'll find a sister branch in Luard Road, Wan Chai, which has a Sunday evening jam session.

➕ F7 ✉ Basement, Mary Building, 71 Peking Road, Tsim Sha Tsui ☎ 2301 3980 🕐 Daily 8am–1am 🚇 Tsim Sha Tsui

HONG KONG CULTURAL CENTRE

hkculturalcentre.gov.hk

At Hong Kong's premier venue for orchestral music, ballet and theater, there's usually an international event of one genre or another on the docket.

➕ E8 ✉ 10 Salisbury Road, Tsim Sha Tsui
☎ 3185 1612 🚇 Tsim Sha Tsui

HONG KONG PHILHARMONIC ORCHESTRA

hkphil.org

The HK Phil, as it's called in Hong Kong, is a large, international orchestra with regular performances, often on weekends, in the Cultural Centre (▷ 67) and City Hall. Ticket prices increase when a prestigious conductor arrives, so plan accordingly.

NED KELLY'S LAST STAND

The best place in Hong Kong for traditional and Dixieland jazz, belted out by a resident band. Expect a convivial atmosphere, pub food and no cover charge.

➕ E7 ✉ 11A Ashley Road, Tsim Sha Tsui
☎ 2376 0562 🕐 Daily 11.30am–2am
🚇 Tsim Sha Tsui

OZONE

ritzcarlton.com/en/hotels/china/hong-kong/dining/ozone

OZONE claims to be the highest bar in the world and few who have perched on the outdoor terrace, 118 floors

---

HOSTESS BARS

Kowloon has plenty of inexpensive, casual bars, many with an Australian flavor, such as Ned Kelly's. There are a few remaining hostess bars, where a drink and a girl to talk to come in a package, but most of these have now closed.

above the city, would argue. The colorful cocktails are super-expensive but it's worth it for the view. No sandals.

🚩 D6 ✉ 118th Floor, Ritz-Carlton Hong Kong, ICC, 1 Austin Road West, Kowloon ☎ 2263 2270 🕐 Mon–Wed 5pm–1am, Thu 5pm–2am, Fri 5pm–3am, Sat 3pm–3am, Sun noon–midnight 🚇 Kowloon

TAP

TAP (The Ale Project) is among the best places to sample local craft beer in the city. Head here to enjoy all the local favorites, plus a few international guest taps to boot. While you're there, sample the tasty pub grub and the sinful sandwiches.

🚩 F3 ✉ 15 Hak Po Street, Mong Kok ☎ 2468 2010 🕐 Mon 4pm–1am, Tue–Thu and Sat noon–1am, Fri noon–2am 🚇 Mong Kok, Exit D3

VIBES

themirahotel.com/dining/vibes/
A well-hidden oasis on the fifth-floor at The Mira hotel, this open-air, exciting bar and music venue feels like you've been transported to Bali. House cocktails and live DJ sets on weekends.

🚩 F7 ✉ 118 Nathan Road, Tsim Sha Tsui, ☎ 2368 1111 🕐 Mon–Wed 6pm–midnight, Thurs–Sat 6pm–1am, Sun 5pm–midnight 🚇 Tsim Sha Tsui, Exit B2

Where to Eat

AQUA ROMA & AQUA TOKYO ($$$)

aqua.com.hk
Located on the top floor of Tsim Tsui's tallest port-front tower (1 Peking Road), Aqua Roma combines Italian cuisine with panoramic views over Victoria Harbour. Aqua Tokyo has a teppanyaki bar and booths overlooking Kowloon's dense cityscape. The Aqua Spirit cocktail bar is just above on the mezzanine floor. Be sure to check the dress code before heading over.

🚩 F7 ✉ 29/F, 1 Peking Road, Tsim Sha Tsui, Kowloon ☎ 3427 2288 🕐 Mon–Sat 12–2.30, 6–11, Sun 12–3, 6–11

AVA RESTAURANT SLASH BAR ($$$)

hotelpanorama.com
This intimate restaurant boasts magnificent Victoria Harbour views. Come here for a cocktail at dusk, or enjoy the global cuisine after dark when the city sparkles. Request a window seat at all costs.

🚩 F7 ✉ 38F, Hotel Panorama, 8A Hart Avenue, Tsim Sha Tsui ☎ 3550 0262 🕐 Daily 6.30am–10.30pm

BOSTONIAN SEAFOOD & GRILL ($$)

langhamhotels.com
Designed to pay tribute to Hong Kong's old shipyards, the renovated restaurant

in the basement of The Langham Hotel promises fresh fish dishes, imported steaks, and cool urban chic decor.

🔲 E7 ✉ Langham Hotel, 8 Peking Road, Tsim Sha Tsui ☎ 2132 7898 🕒 Daily 12–3, 6.30–11 🚇 Tsim Sha Tsui

DELHI CLUB ($)

The Delhi Club is plush by Chungking Mansions standards and frequented by many regulars—two good reasons for a feast here.

🔲 F7 ✉ Block C, Flat 3, 3rd Floor, Chungking Mansions, 36–44 Nathan Road, Tsim Sha Tsui ☎ 2368 1682 🕒 Daily 12–3.30, 6–11.30 🚇 Tsim Sha Tsui

DIN TAI FUNG ($–$$)

dintaifung.com.hk

The Tsim Sha Tsui outlet of this ever-popular Taiwanese nationwide chain has remarkably earned itself a Michelin star. It's the best place in town to try *xiao-longbao*, Shanghai's much-loved broth-filled pork dumplings. Expect to queue on weekends and at lunch time, but it's worth the wait.

🔲 E8 ✉ Shop 310, 3rd Floor, Silvercord Centre, 30 Canton Road, Tsim Sha Tsui ☎ 2730 6928 🕒 Daily noon–midnight 🚇 Tsim Sha Tsui

FELIX ($$–$$$)

peninsula.com/en/hong-kong/hotel-fine-dining/felix

You'll find excellent contemporary pan-Asian cuisine in this chic, modern restaurant, artfully styled by French designer, Philippe Starck. The night city view from the wrap-around floor-to-ceiling windows is magical and not to be missed.

🔲 F8 ✉ 28th Floor, Peninsula Hotel, Salisbury Road, Kowloon ☎ 2696 6778 🕒 Daily 6pm–10.30pm 🚇 Tsim Sha Tsui

GADDI'S ($$$)

peninsula.com/en/hong-kong/hotel-fine-dining/gaddis-french-restaurant

One of Hong Kong's best restaurants is somewhere you'll remember, especially if you go at night when the chandeliers are sparkling and the band is playing. It's popular with tourists and locals alike for both its fine service and French food. Reservations are a must.

🔲 F8 ✉ 1st Floor, Peninsula Hotel, Salisbury Road, Tsim Sha Tsui ☎ 2696 6763 🕒 Daily 12–3, 6.30–11 🚇 Tsim Sha Tsui

GAYLORD INDIAN RESTAURANT ($)

mayfare.com.hk

The starters here are superb, and the breads and kebabs come fresh out of the tandoori oven. One of the best ways to try the food here is to have a lunch buffet. Cozy and pubby.

🔲 E7 ✉ 1st Floor, Ashley Centre, 23–25 Ashley Road, Tsim Sha Tsui ☎ 2376 1001 🕒 Daily 12–2.30, 6–11 🚇 Tsim Sha Tsui

GREEN COMMON ($)

greencommon.com

A top choice for vegetarians and vegans, Green Common combines a plant-based grocery and a buzzing café. Carnivores enjoy it too, thanks to plant-based meat substitutes like the savory

---

DRINKS

For decent coffee, look to the European- and American-style coffee booths in glitzy shopping malls. Cafés and hotel restaurants are your best bet if you're looking for a proper English tea served with fresh milk and sugar. Foreign beers and local craft brews are readily available—Moonzen, Young Master Ales or Gweilo. Western wine is available in most restaurants.

Beyond Burger, Beyond Sausage and Omnipork dumplings.

🔹 E7 ✉ Shop OT, G/F, Ocean Terminal, Harbour City, 17 Canton Road, Tsim Sha Tsui ☎ 3102 1220 🕐 Daily noon–9.30pm 🚇 Tsim Sha Tsui

HARLAN'S ($$$)

jcgroup.hk/restaurants/harlans

A fine-dining restaurant atop Hong Kong's tallest shopping mall. The indoor dining space is pleasant, but the stand-out draw is without question the wonderful balcony with views the length of Nathan Road to the harbor. Fare is mainly Mediterranean.

🔹 F7 ✉ Level 19, The ONE, 100 Nathan Road, Tsim Sha Tsui ☎ 2972 2222 🕐 Daily 12–2.30, 6–12.30 🚇 Tsim Sha Tsui

KHYBER PASS ($)

If you are keen to venture into Chungking Mansions (▷ 109 panel), this 7th-floor mess hall is a good place to start your adventure. Seating is at long tables, prices are low and the north Indian food is pretty standard.

🔹 F7 ✉ 7th Floor, Block E, Chungking Mansions, Nathan Road ☎ 2721 2786 🕐 Daily noon–3.30, 6–11.30 🚇 Tsim Sha Tsui

MAZE GRILL ($$$)

diningconcepts.com/restaurants/maze-grill

One of the latest openings in Hong Kong by acclaimed chef Gordon Ramsay, Maze Grill is set inside Harbour City mall, but don't let the commercial location throw you off. This is one of the best places in Hong Kong to dig into indulgent steaks and traditional English dishes such as beef Wellington and sticky toffee pudding.

🔹 F7 ✉ Harbour City Shop, OTE401, Level 4, Ocean Terminal, Tsim Sha Tsui ☎ 2765 0890 🕐 Daily 11.30–11 🚇 Tsim Sha Tsui, Exit L6

MEZZO ($$)

regalhotel.com

American-style steaks and seafood. The restaurant specializes in chargrilled dishes. Try the sole fillets wrapped in applewood smoked bacon.

🔹 F7 ✉ Regal Kowloon Hotel, 71 Mody Road, Tsim Sha Tsui ☎ 2313 8778 🕐 Daily 12–3, 6–11 🚇 Tsim Sha Tsui

MING COURT ($$$)

cordishotels.com

For Michelin-starred Cantonese fare and a swish environment, head to Ming Court at Cordis Hotel in Mong Kok. The Champagne-hued interiors augur well for what's to come: dainty dim sum, delectable seafood, and premium Chinese teas.

🔹 F3 ✉ 555 Shanghai Street, Mong Kok, Kowloon ☎ 3552 3028 🕐 Daily 11–2.30, 6–10.30 🚇 Mong Kok

NADAMAN ($$$)

shangri-la.com

The interior design at Nadaman is simple yet sophisticated, with a definite Japanese feel. There is a sushi bar available or you could reserve one of the booth tables for a more intimate meal. The extensive menu offers quality sushi, sashimi and tempura as well as other authentic Japanese cuisine. A chef's set menu is also available.

🔹 F7 ✉ Basement Floor 2, Kowloon Shangri-La, 64 Mody Road, Tsim Sha Tsui ☎ 2733 8751 🕐 Daily noon–2.30, 6.30–10.30 🚇 East Tsim Sha Tsui KCR, Tsim Sha Tsui MTR

RECH BY ALAIN DUCASSE ($$$$)

hongkong-ic.intercontinental.com

Awash in soft whites and oceanic hues, Rech is a fresh concept by French chef Alain Ducasse. Sitting pretty inside the InterContinental Hotel, the restaurant

specializes in rustic seafood dishes and home-made desserts.

🔲 F7 ✉ Lobby Level, InterContinental Hong Kong, 18 Salisbury Road, Tsim Sha Tsui ☎ 2313 2323 🕐 Daily 6–11pm 🚇 Tsim Sha Tsui

SAGANO RESTAURANT ($$$)

newworldmillenniumhotel.com

The Japanese chefs at this restaurant in a Japanese hotel prepare distinctive kansai cuisine from around the Kyoto area. Don't miss the teppanyaki counter, where the chefs create intricate delicacies whilst juggling with their sharp cooking tools.

🔲 G7 ✉ 1st Floor, New World Millennium Hong Kong Hotel, 72 Mody Road, Tsim Sha Tsui ☎ 2313 4215 🕐 Daily 12–2.30, 6–10.30 🚇 Tsim Sha Tsui

SHIKIGIKU JAPANESE RESTAURANT ($$)

rghk.com.hk/dining

World-renowned tempura, sushi, teppanyaki and sashimi is served in this chic and quietly elegant restaurant located on the first floor of the luxury Royal Garden Hotel. There is free parking available for diners.

🔲 E7 ✉ 69 Mody Road, Tsim Sha Tsui East, Kowloon ☎ 2733 2933 🕐 Daily 12–3, 6–11 🚇 Tsim Sha Tsui

THEO MISTRAL BY THEO RANDALL ($$$)

hongkong.intercontinental.com

Enjoy a relaxed meal away from the Tsim Sha Tsui crowds, plus excellent pasta, pizza and other Italian dishes. Rustic Mediterranean furnishings.

🔲 G4 ✉ Basement Floor 2, Grand Stanford InterContinental, 70 Mody Road, Tsim Sha Tsui East ☎ 2721 5161 🕐 Daily noon–2.30, 6–10.30 🚇 Tsim Sha Tsui

WOODLANDS INTERNATIONAL RESTAURANT ($)

woodlandshk.com

One of the city's best Indian vegetarian restaurants, the decor is slightly spartan but the food is excellent. The *dosa* (rice-flour pancakes) and *thali* (set meals) are excellent and good value. Note: no alcohol is served here.

🔲 F7 ✉ Upper Ground Floor, Wing On Plaza, 62 Mody Road, Tsim Sha Tsui ☎ 2369 3718 🕐 Daily 12–3.30, 6.30–10.30 🚇 Tsim Sha Tsui

YAN TOH HEEN ($$$)

hongkong-ic.intercontinental.com

Travelers can enjoy excellent, upscale Cantonese cuisine directly on the waterfront at this prestigious eatery. The restaurant is located on the ground floor of the InterContinental Hote, and features gorgeous place settings in green jade. There is a special tea gallery as well as excellent harborside views. Yan Toh Heen has won lots of awards for its cooking and ambience over the years, making it a great choice for business lunches, date nights and family celebrations. On weekends, head here for dim sum.

🔲 F8 ✉ InterContinental Hotel, 18 Salisbury Road, Tsim Sha Tsui ☎ 2313 2323 🕐 Mon–Sat 12–2.30, 6–11, Sun 11.30–3, 6–11 🚇 Tsim Sha Tsui

---

VEGETARIAN CHOICE

Vegetarian diners in Hong Kong are rarely disappointed, especially as there are many vegetarian options offered in the Buddhist, Sri Lankan, South Indian and North Indian restaurants found throughout the city. A few vegetable curries accompanied by *raita* (yogurt) and *naan* (puffed-up whole wheat), complemented by a lentil *dal* is a small feast for two.

New Territories

The vast bulk of the Special Administrative Region stretches across the rural hinterland north of Kowloon. The countryside is studded with new towns and traditional villages, as well as parks, walking trails, wetlands, ancient temples and museums.

Top 25

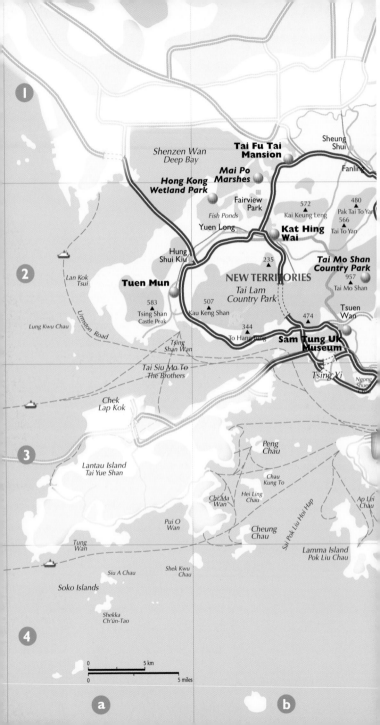

Hong Kong Wetland Park

HIGHLIGHTS

● Pui Pui, the celebrity crocodile
● The views across the wetlands from the viewing gallery
● The wobbly mangrove boardwalk

TIPS

● The website's planner page makes your trip more productive.
● There is an indoor children's play area.

Home to an incredible array of flora and fauna, this huge artificial wetland area stretches across 60 hectares. The park now offers to visitors an accessible and entertaining view of the colorful and varied wildlife of the Mai Po Marshes.

Wetland ecology Hong Kong's striking natural scenery and its diverse outdoor attractions often take travelers by surprise—and the Wetland Park is no exception. Situated between the Mai Po Marshes (▷ 85) and the scarily large Tin Shui Wai New Town, this vast wetland, covering some 151 acres (61ha), stands as a barrier protecting the marshes from encroachment by the town and a means by which locals and visitors alike can learn about the diverse ecology of the wetlands.

Clockwise from left: A fishpond and hide; exploring the Wetland Park on the wooden boardwalks; Pui Pui the crocodile; a black-faced spoonbill

The Wetland Interactive World The visitor center's exhibits provide information about the world's various wetlands and the impact humans have on them. The theater offers a global perspective, while the viewing gallery allows visitors to see the wetlands through telescopes and cameras located around the park.

On the boardwalks Outside, four wooden boardwalks lead visitors around the various habitats of the park: Through areas planted to attract specific insects, birds, butterflies, dragonflies and mangrove dwellers, to areas for creatures that live and hunt in the streams. A boardwalk crosses mangroves and there are three hides where you can watch the wildlife without being seen. The reserve is home to a crocodile called Pui Pui.

THE BASICS

wetlandpark.gov.hk

b2

Wetland Park Road, Tin Shui Wai

3152 2666

Mon, Wed–Sun 10–5

Café on ground floor

Tin Shui Wai (MTR) then light rail 705 Tin Shui Wai Circular to Wetland Park Station

The center is accessible but boardwalks could be difficult

Moderate

Shop

Ten Thousand Buddhas Monastery

- Thousands of small statues of Buddha
- Embalmed and gilded body of monastery's founder
- Statues of Buddha's followers
- Views over Sha Tin

- Do not use flash photography inside the monastery.
- Look out for wild macaques on the way up.

A half-hour train ride out of Hong Kong brings you to this striking temple set on a hillside overlooking the apartments, housing projects and towers of the satellite town of Sha Tin.

Bountiful Buddhas To reach the monastery, take the train to Sha Tin and follow the signs. You must then climb 431 steps up the hillside. Every five steps or so is a life-size fiberglass Buddha. At the top, you'll find a beautiful temple that was built between 1949 and 1957. Known locally as Man Fat Sze Temple, this Buddhist shrine has become known as the Ten Thousand Buddhas Temple because of the matrix of small statues that decorate it. The statues are all different—some black, some covered in gold leaf—and each Buddha strikes

There are actually many more than 10,000 gold plated Buddha statues placed throughout this monastery

a different pose. There are actually 13,000 or more Buddhas—but who's counting?

Panoramas and pagodas From the edge of the courtyard there are magnificent views over Sha Tin. The courtyard houses a tiered pagoda and the statues of some of Buddha's bright red followers, as well as several temples and pavilions. On the route up to the temple is another set of four temples, one containing Hong Kong's second-tallest Buddha statue, another the embalmed, gilded remains of Yuet Kai, who founded the Man Fat Sze Monastery and, despite his great age, personally carried some of the stones up to the site from the bottom of the hill. If there is a funeral taking place here, you will see paper gifts that are burned for the deceased in the afterlife.

THE BASICS

10kbuddhas.org
(in Chinese)

➕ c2

✉ Close to Pai Tau Street, Sha Tin, New Territories

☎ 2691 1067

🕐 Daily 9–6. Particularly busy around Chinese New Year

🚇 Sha Tin

♿ None

💵 Free, but donations welcome

Wong Tai Sin Temple

TOP 25

Wong Tai Sin Temple (left) and a streetside stand at the temple (right)

THE BASICS

siksikyuen.org.hk

⊕ c3

✉ Wong Tai Sin Estate; follow signs from MTR station

☎ Information: 2327 8141

🕐 Daily 7–5. Main temple is not always accessible

🚇 Wong Tai Sin (exit 82)

♿ Good

🎫 Free (donations welcomed)

HIGHLIGHTS

● Main altar including painting of Wong Tai Sin
● Garden of Nine Dragon Wall
● Fortune-telling arcade
● Clinic block
● Stands outside selling windmills and hell money
● Chinese gardens at rear of complex
● Side altar in main temple dedicated to monkey god
● Incinerators for burning offerings

If temples were shops, then Wong Tai Sin Temple would be a supermarket. During Chinese New Year, hundreds of devotees wave joss sticks as they whirl from one deity to the next.

Wong Tai Sin This large Taoist temple, built in 1973 in a Chinese style and situated among high-rise residential blocks, is dedicated to Wong Tai Sin, an ex-shepherd who was taught how to cure all ills by a passing deity. Today, Wong Tai Sin is a very popular god, as he is in charge of the fortunes of gamblers. He can also be sought out by those who are ill or who have concerns about their health, and by people asking for help in business matters.

Symbolic interior The temple complex is vast, almost stadium-size, composed not just of the main temple, where Wong Tai Sin is represented by a painting rather than a statue, but also by turtle ponds, libraries, medicine halls and what is almost a small shopping mall of fortune-tellers. The temple is built to represent the geomantic elements of gold, wood, water, fire and earth. In the Yue Heung Shrine are fire and earth; gold is represented in the Bronze Luen Pavilion where the portrait of Wong Tai Sin is kept; and the Library Hall and water fountain represent wood and water respectively. The temple also caters to those who venerate Confucius, represented in the Confucius Hall, while Buddhists come here to worship the Buddhist goddess of mercy, Kuan Yin.

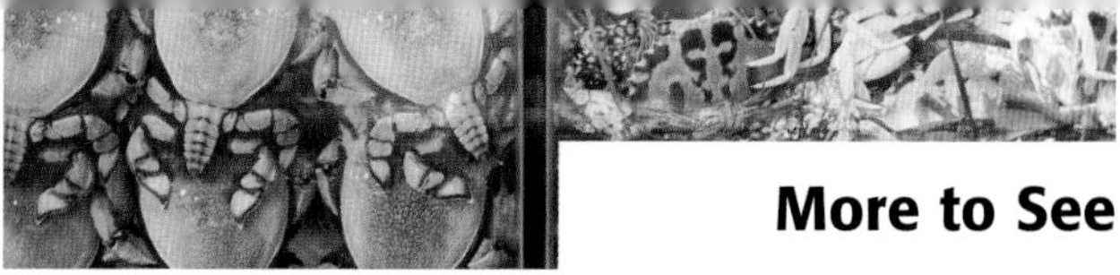

More to See

CHI LIN NUNNERY

chilin.org

Where the nearby Wong Tai Sin Temple (opposite) is always hectic, Chi Lin Nunnery offers a place of calm, largely thanks to the beautifully landscaped Nan Lian Garden. In 1990, the complex was rebuilt in the style of a palatial Tang dynasty complex, but it looks ancient: The all-timber nunnery buildings were even built without the use of a single metal hinge or nail, making it a highly photogenic stop.

�" c3 ✉ 5 Chi Lin Drive, Diamond Hill, Kowloon ☎ 2354 1888 🕓 Daily 9–4.30; Garden 6.30am–7pm 🚇 Diamond Hill MTR (exit C2) 🎟 Free ♿ Poor

KAT HING WAI

The biggest of Hong Kong's clans, the Tangs, settled here hundreds of years ago, building walled villages as protection against bandits and pirates. Four hundred Hakka still inhabit the village of Kat Hing Wai.

�" b2 ✉ Kam Tin 🚇 Kam Sheung Road MTR ♿ Poor

MAI PO MARSHES

On the edge of mainland China and framed by the hazy, fume-filled skyline of Shenzhen, the internationally protected Mai Po Marshes are home to thousands of rare and endangered birds—get some binoculars to view.

�" b1 ✉ Mai Po ☎ 2526 1011 🕓 Daily 9–6 🚇 Sheung Shui then a taxi 🚌 76K from Sheung Shui MTR station ♿ None 🎟 Moderate ❓ Reserve a visit in advance since numbers are limited. Refundable deposit required. Binoculars can be rented at the visitor center

SAI KUNG PENINSULA

This is the green lung of Hong Kong, containing the 18,772-acre (7,600ha) Ma On Shan Country Park, a reservoir, the Maclehose walking trail, a marine park and the fourth highest peak in the territory. Start at Sai Kung village, and go island hopping or walk the trails.

�" d2 🚇 MTR to Sha Tin then bus 299X to Sai Kung village or MTR to Diamond Hill then bus 92

The Sai Kung Peninsula

Women of Kat Hing Wai in traditional Hakka dress

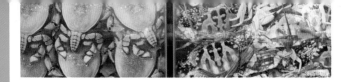

SAM TUNG UK MUSEUM

heritagemuseum.gov.hk

The simple lines of this ancient Hakka village stand out against the forest of high-rise housing blocks. The main hall is highly ornate and colorful. The other two halls, used for daily living, are more rustic and display everyday farming tools.

🚹 b2 ✉ 2 Kwu Uk Lane, Tsuen Wan, New Territories ☎ 2411 2001 🕐 Mon, Wed–Sun 10–6 🚇 Tsuen Wan (exit E) ♿ Few 🎫 Free 🛈 HKTB Heritage tour, plus private tours

SHA TIN

Sha Tin is easily visited by train from Kowloon. In addition to a huge shopping and entertainment complex, there are restaurants, temples, Hong Kong's second horse-racing track, mountain trails and a Tang walled village. Look out for the fountain opposite the station with its pretty display of water and sparkling lights.

🚹 c2 🍴 Many, especially in New Town Plaza 🚇 Sha Tin MTR ♿ Good

TAI FU TAI MANSION

lcsd.gov.hk/CE/Museum/Monument/en/monuments_32.php

Built around 1865, this traditional mansion has been fully and beautifully restored; ceramic figurines decorate the facade, while the many rooms contain plaster moldings and woodcarvings.

🚹 b1 ✉ Wing Ping, Tsuen, San Tin, Yuen Long 🕐 Mon, Wed and Sun 9–1, 2–5 🚌 Sheung Shui MTR then bus 76K

TAI MO SHAN COUNTRY PARK

afcd.gov.hk

This country park is home to Hong Kong's highest mountain and the beautiful Ng Tung Chai waterfalls.

🚹 b2 ✉ Tsuen Wan 🍴 Take a picnic 🚇 Tsuen Wan 🎫 Free

TUEN MUN

Several interesting and historic Buddhist and Taoist monasteries can be found in Tuen Mun, such as Castle Peak, Ching Chung Koon and Miu Fat.

🚹 a2 🚇 Tuen Mun MTR West

Red altar in the Sam Tung Uk Museum

To Ten Thousand Buddhas Monastery

This walk from Che Kung to the Ten Thousand Buddhas Monastery goes via a shopping megatropolis in Sha Tin.

DISTANCE: 2.2 miles (3.5km) **ALLOW:** 2 hours (plus shopping time)

START

CHE KUNG TEMPLE MTR
🚇 c2 🚈 Che Kung Temple KCR

1 Leave the station (on the Ma On Shan line) by Exit B and go through the pedestrian subway crossing Che Kung Miu Road. Turn right and walk for 10 minutes.

2 At the Che Kung Temple be sure to turn the windmills for good luck. Che Kung, who protects against floods, stands dark red and shiny in the center of the temple.

3 Retrace your steps along Che Kung Miu Road to the pedestrian tunnel and follow signs to Tsang Tai Uk. This will lead you through a number of pedestrian tunnels.

4 You will know you have emerged at the right place when you see tennis courts on your left. The village of Tsang Tai Uk is now almost derelict.

END

TEN THOUSAND BUDDHAS MONASTERY
(▷ 82–83) 🚇 c2 🚈 Sha Tin KCR

8 At the MTR barriers turn right to exit New Town Plaza. At the bus terminal, turn left and head right and downward, then turn left through Pau Tai village. Here, turn right to reach the monastery.

7 Farther along, Lek Yuen bridge is on the right. Turn left here and climb the steps of the registry office to a podium. Cross to the walkway leading past Snoopy's World to New Town Plaza. Make your way to the MTR.

6 Use the subway to cross Lion Rock Road to Sha Tin Park opposite. Follow the river and exit the park through the north gate, passing the amphitheater on the right.

5 Return to the pedestrian tunnels. This time follow signs to the Hong Kong Heritage Museum to take you over the Lion Bridge across the Shing Mun river channel.

NEW TERRITORIES WALK

Shopping

SHA TIN

If you are looking for imported foods, snacks, and Japanese products, you might also try Yata department store in New Town Plaza. There are lots of reasonably priced clothes shops too. If you prefer to shop without the crowds, make sure you don't go on a Sunday, or you will find yourself knocking elbows with what seems like the entire population of the New Territories.

➕ C2 🍴 Restaurants in New Town Plaza
🚇 Sha Tin MTR

TAI PO MARKET

Tai Po is a colorful and busy blend of malls, street markets and museums. The hub remains Fu Shin Street, where stalls sell everything and anything from inexpensive clothing to cooking utensils and herbal remedies. Meanwhile, the MTR station which takes the same name is surrounded by the immense Uptown Plaza, if you want a more serene shopping experience.

➕ C2 ✉ Fu Shin Street ⏰ Fu Shin Street Market 10–10; Wet market 6am–9pm
🚇 Tai Wo MTR

Entertainment and Nightlife

CLEARWATER BAY GOLF AND COUNTRY CLUB

cwbgolf.org

A par-70, 18-hole, pro-championship course. Visitors allowed weekday mornings; a handicap certificate is required.

➕ C3 ✉ 139 Tai Mun Road, Clearwater Bay ☎ 2719 1595 ⏰ Daily 7am–9pm 🚇 Hang Hau 💰 Green fees HK$100–250 per round

KAU SAI CHAU PUBLIC GOLF COURSE

kscgolf.org.hk

Here (opposite), there are three 18-hole courses and a driving range.

➕ d2 ✉ Kau Sai Chau, Sai Kung, New Territories ☎ 2791 3388 ⏰ Fri, Sat, Sun 7am–10pm 🚇 Choi Hung, then bus 92 or

Green Minibus No. 1A to Sai Kung Bus Terminal. Go to waterfront for the golf course's ferry for Kau Sai Chau 💰 Green fees HK$620–HK$960

SHA TIN TOWN HALL

lcsd.gov.hk/stth

The Town Hall hosts many international artists, especially classical orchestras.

➕ C2 ✉ 1 Yeun Wo Road, New Town Plaza, Sha Tin ☎ 2694 2509 ⏰ Daily 9am–11pm 🚇 Sha Tin MTR

SILVERSTRAND

This stretch of sand is one of three excellent swimming beaches with changing rooms and food stalls.

➕ C3 ✉ Clearwater Bay Road, Sai Kung 🚇 Choi Hung then bus 92 or taxi

Where to Eat

PRICES

Prices are approximate, based on a 3-course meal for one person.

$$$	over HK$700
$$	HK$300–HK$700
$	under HK$300

AH POR TOFU FA ($)

A little spot in Tai Po, Ah Por Tofu Fa (meaning "Tofu Granny") serves HK$8 tofu puddings. Few seats are available but locals eat the popular Chinese dessert as a quick snack while standing.

➕ c1 ✉ Shop 2A, Tai Kwong Lane, Tai Po ☎ No phone 🕐 Daily 9.30–8 💵 Cash only 🚇 Tai Po Market MTR

ANTHONY'S RANCH ($$)

anthonys-ranch.com

Specializing in Texas smoke-house cuisine, this expat-friendly restaurant majors in ribs, burgers, steaks and chops. You can look forward to bands on weekends and televized sports.

➕ Off map c2 ✉ Ground Floor, 28 Yi Chun Street, Sai Kung ☎ 2791 6113 🕐 Mon–Thu 11am–midnight, Fri 11–4am, Sat 8am–4am, Sun 8am–midnight 🚇 Choi Hung MTR (exit C2) then 1A minibus

FU LUM FUSION ($$)

This Chinese restaurant in New Town Plaza is an upgraded version of Fu Lum restaurants around the city. You'll find fun and modern plating while still serving traditional Chinese dishes.

➕ c2 ✉ Shop 9A–9B, 2/F, Wai Wah Centre, 11–17 Centre Street, Sha Tin ☎ 2570 0168 🕐 Daily 10am–11pm 🚇 Sha Tin MTR

SAKURADA ($$)

royalpark.com.hk

At this classy Japanese place in the Royal Park Hotel, the food is prepared by Japanese chefs. Teppanyaki is a specialty, so don't leave without trying it.

➕ c2 ✉ 8 Pak Hok Ting Street, Sha Tin ☎ 2694 3810 🕐 Daily 11.30–3, 6–11 🚇 Sha Tin MTR

SHA TIN 18 ($$$)

hyatt.com

Inside the Hyatt Regency Hong Kong, Sha Tin 18 is one of the best places to try Peking duck. The crispy skin and juicy meat comes with all the extras—think steamy pancake wraps, celery, scallions, hoisin sauce and sugar.

➕ c2 ✉ 18 Chak Cheung Street, Ma Liu Shui, Sha Tin ☎ 3723 7932 🕐 Daily 11.30–3, 5.30–10.30pm 🚇 University, Exit B MTR

LA TERRAZZA BAR AND GRILL ($$)

luprarestaurant.com./hongkong/terrazza.cfm

Located amid the rooftop greenery of Sha Tin Town Hall, La Terrazza is one of the few upscale Western restaurants in this part of Hong Kong. It's not overly posh, despite the beautiful location, and the set lunches offer a decent value.

➕ c2 ✉ Roof Garden, Sha Tin Town Hall, 1 Yuen Wo Road, Sha Tin ☎ 2940 2827 🕐 Mon–Fri noon–11, Sat–Sun 11–11 🚇 Sha Tin MTR

TUNG KEE SEAFOOD RESTAURANT ($–$$)

tungkee.com.hk

This popular Sai Kung restaurant is on the promenade and offers plenty of outdoor tables for seaside dining. The restaurant does great set meals for groups of two or more. You can also find a second restaurant outlet on Hoi Pong Square.

➕ c2 ✉ 96–102 Man Nin Street, Sai Kung ☎ 2792 7453 🕐 Daily 4.30am–10.30pm 🚇 Diamond Hill MTR, then KMB bus service 92

Farther Afield

Encircling Hong Kong Island are 260 or more outlying islands, many of them little more than uninhabited rocks, but several make for an exciting day out. One, of course, is home to the Tian Tan Buddha.

Top 25

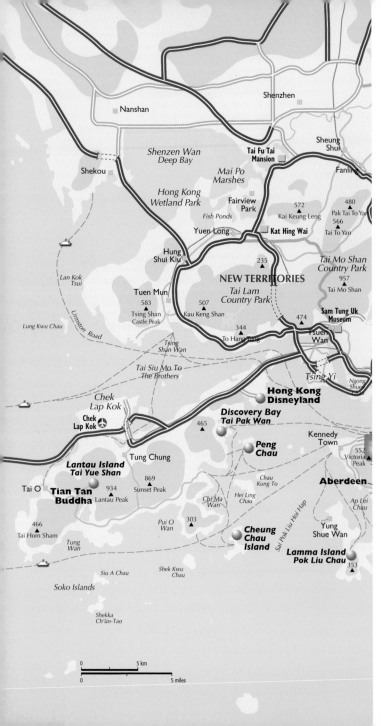

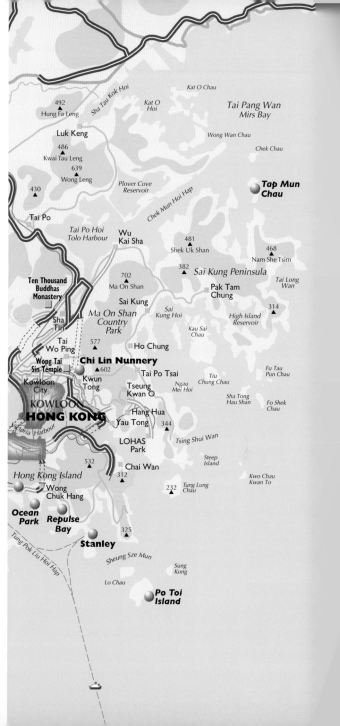

Cheung Chau Island

Cheung Chau has two beautiful beaches, dozens of seafood restaurants, interesting temples, caves, a windsurfing center, bicycles for rent, good walks and an annual bun festival.

Ferry to Cheung Chau The air-conditioned, 35-minute fast ferry ride past speeding catamarans, scruffy sampans, vast tankers and tiny golden islands is a hassle-free experience. You could spend a couple of days on this car-free island, enjoying its beaches, eating seafood and wandering the footpaths. Cheung Chau is great for scenic walks along paved paths (watch out for the little electric vehicles that cart goods around the island). To the north, a route leads you uphill to a reservoir from where there are excellent views over the island.

Clockwise from left: Pak Tai Temple entrance; stone carving Pak Tai Temple; one of the open-air seafood restaurants on the island; beautiful sunset on Cheung Chau; fresh fish is a staple of the island; overlooking the bay at Cheung Chau

To the south, another road brings you to Sai Wan village where there is a Tin Hau temple and a footpath to the cave (so the story goes) of a pirate called Cheung Po-Tsai. From Sai Wan you can catch a 10-minute sampan boat back to Cheung Chau village, a fun trip in itself.

The village In Cheung Chau village there are a few things to see and quite a lot to eat. Cheung Chau's main draw is the modern Pak Tai Temple (originally built in the 18th century), dedicated to the god who saved the island from plague. Each year the bun festival, which takes place over a week in summer, brings in thousands of visitors. There is a vibrant market selling seafood, vegetables and freshwater pearls to the 20,000 or so residents. Be sure to leave time for a good wander around the side streets.

THE BASICS

- ✚ See map ▷ 92–93
- 🚢 Outlying Islands Pier 5, Central: approximately half-hourly 24 hours (only three ferries run between midnight and 6.10am)
- ♿ Difficult
- 🍴 Moderate
- ❓ Tung Wan and Kwun Yam beaches have cafés

Tian Tan Buddha and Lantau Island

HIGHLIGHTS

● Tian Tan Buddha
● Tranquil monastery
● Views of the South China Sea and other islands
● Ngong Ping 360
● Museum of Buddha's life (podium, 2nd level)

TIP

● Hong Kong Dolphin Watch (hkdolphinwatch. com) organizes trips to see the endangered pink dolphins of Lantau island every Monday, Friday and Sunday.

The 112ft-tall (34m), 250-ton bronze statue of Buddha on Lantau Island can be seen in his meditative pose from your aircraft as you descend into Chek Lap Kok airport.

Worth the trek Even after the airport was built, Lantau remained one of the largest green areas in Hong Kong. It is home to rare species such as the Hong Kong newt and the ayu, a stream-dwelling fish. This isolated outpost is also home to almost 300 Buddhist monasteries, most of them tiny temples tucked away in remote areas. Po Lin (Precious Lotus) Monastery, half-way up the mountainside on the Ngong Ping Plateau was established by three monks in 1905 and is regularly restored, most recently in 2013. The monastery's major attraction is the

The gigantic bronze Tian Tan Buddha is a truly amazing sight

famous Tian Tan Buddha, completed in 1993, on the hilltop above the monastery. To get up close, you need to climb 268 steps. At the summit, you will be rewarded with a splendid view of Lantau.

Footpaths and beaches There are miles of challenging and unspoiled footpaths on the island, as well as some pretty beaches: The most accessible beaches are on the eastern shores, the most accessible at Mui Wo, where the ferries from Central dock. On the south coast, head to Pui O and Cheung Sha, both easily reached from Mui Wo by bus.

Cable car ride An essential part of the Lantau experience is the Ngong Ping 360 cable car trip—the 3.5-mile (5.7km) ride is spectacular.

THE BASICS

plm.org.hk
➕ See map ▷ 92–93
✉ Lantau Island
🕐 Monastery: daily 8–6.
Ngong Ping 360: Mon–Fri 10–6, Sat–Sun 9–6.30.
Tian Tan Big Buddha: Monday to Sunday 10-5.30
🚇 Tung Chung and then bus 23 heading for Po Lin or Skyrail cable-car
🚢 Ferry to Mui Wo from Outlying Ferry Pier 6 (journey time approx 45 min), then bus 2
💵 Free. Skyrail moderate
❓ HKTB guided walks: Lantau Island–Tung Chung Valley

More to See

DISCOVERY BAY

Known locally as "DB," this is a community of apartment-block dwellers, most of whom commute daily to Hong Kong Island. They enjoy car-free living and a stretch of white-sand beaches. There are restaurants, shops and facilities including the Discovery Bay Golf Club, plus hiking trails of Lantau. A catamaran takes about 25 minutes from Central or buses connect with Tung Chung MTR.

✛ See map ▷ 92–93 ⛴ Air-conditioned round-the-clock ferries take 25 min from Central

HONG KONG DISNEYLAND

hongkongdisneyland.com

Meet all of your favorite Disney characters in Fantasyland, sail into darkest Africa and Asia on Adventureland's Jungle River Cruise and take a flight on a soaring space adventure in Tomorrowland. Hong Kong Disneyland is on Lantau Island and offers a great day out for young and old alike. There are seven main areas to explore, each offering thrilling experiences, from climbing Tarzan's Treehouse to hurtling at speed into the universe on Space Mountain.

✛ See map ▷ 92–93 ⊙ Daily 10.30–8 🚇 Tung Chung line from Hong Kong station, then Disneyland resort line at Sunny Bay 💷 Expensive (savings can be had at off-peak times)

LAMMA ISLAND

A short ferry ride from the city, Lamma Island is car-free and offers a relaxing day out in relatively unspoiled countryside. Most people who visit do one of the pretty, moderately simple walks and end their day with dinner in one of the island's popular seafood restaurants. Ferries arrive at the island's biggest village, Yung Shue Wan, at the northwestern end of the island. There are restaurants, a bank, post office and Tin Hau temple here.

From Yung Shue Wan an hour-long, easy walk across the island brings you to Sok Kwu Wan (also

Gazing out to sea from Lamma Island

accessible by ferry from Central), where the bulk of the seafood restaurants are located.

Another half-hour walk from Yung Shue Wan brings you to Mo Tat Wan, a tiny village, and the nearby beaches of Shek Pai Wan and Sham Wan. From Sok Kwu Wan a path leads you to the highest point on the island, Mount Stenhouse.

➕ See map ▷ 92–93 🖼️ Outlying Islands Pier 4, Central to Yung Shue Wan: half-hourly 6.30am–12.30am. Last returning ferry at 11.30pm. From Central to Sok Kwu Wan: 7.30am–11.30pm. Last returning ferry is 10.40pm 🎟️ Free ♿ Poor

PENG CHAU

This small island to the east of Lantau is popular with day-trippers. Climb to the island's highest point, Finger Hill, at 311ft (95m), visit an 18th-century Tin Hau temple, explore the shops in the narrow lanes or sample the seafood in one of the restaurants. Five minutes from the village is Tung Wan, the island's only beach.

Tin Hau Temple, Peng Chau Island

➕ See map ▷ 92–93 🖼️ Inexpensive seafood restaurants in village 🖼️ Outlying Islands Ferry Pier 6, Central: 7am–12.30am. Last ferry back at 11.30pm

PO TOI ISLAND

Although close to Hong Kong Island, this tiny rocky place is one of the least accessible of the islands. Ferries run only on weekends but you cannot stay on Po Toi. It is possible to visit during the week if you hire a junk. The island has a Tin Hau temple and lots of walks. It takes about two hours to walk right round the island. Po Toi is popular with picnickers on Sunday who come for the walks and for the Bronze Age rock carving. There are a few seafood restaurants and a little beach at Tai Wan where the ferry docks. An excellent website (hkoutdoors.com) details a fine walk across the island.

➕ See map ▷ 92–93 🖼️ Kaito Ferries operate from St. Stephen's Beach, near Stanley, on Sat, Sun. Ferries also run between Aberdeen and Po Toi on Tue, Thu, Sat, Sun and public holidays

TAP MUN CHAU

A tiny island off the Sai Kung Peninsula, Tap Mun Chau has a few scattered inhabitants who make their living from fishing. There are many pleasant walks and some sandy beaches with clean water for swimming. There's a Tin Hau temple, some semi-wild cows and bird life make up all there is to see. On weekdays you'll have the island to yourself.

➕ See map ▷ 92–93 🖼️ 2 ferries a day (3 Sat and Sun) from Ma Liu Shui Pier, near University MTR station. Last ferry: 5.30pm

Lantau Island

A walk across Lantau Island from Po Lin across natural woodlands, stark hillsides and a verdant valley to the new town of Tung Chung.

DISTANCE: 4.3 miles (7km) **ALLOW:** 3 hours

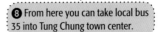

START

TIAN TAN BUDDHA (▷ 96–97)
🚇 Tung Chung and then buses or cable car for Po Lin

END

TUNG CHUNG
🚇 Tung Chung

❶ From the bottom of the Big Buddha steps follow the sign for the Tea Garden. From there follow signs for the Wisdom Path. At a crossroads divert to the right to the Wisdom Path, a series of wooden obelisks marking out the infinity symbol.

❽ From here you can take local bus 35 into Tung Chung town center.

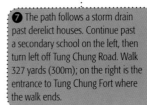

❷ Return to the crossroads and go straight across, following a fenced, level pathway through trees. Many of the plants growing here are labeled in Latin and English.

❼ The path follows a storm drain past derelict houses. Continue past a secondary school on the left, then turn left off Tung Chung Road. Walk 327 yards (300m); on the right is the entrance to Tung Chung Fort where the walk ends.

❸ At the end of the path turn briefly on to a wide concrete path leading through a gateway decorated with calligraphy and pink knobs signposted to Tung Chung via Tei Tong Tsai.

❻ The path joins a concrete road. Turn right onto the road and find another concrete archway set into a wall on the left. Turn through the archway, passing beehives and banana trees. You'll see high-rise apartments in view ahead.

❹ The path winds downward through trees and ferns. About 0.6 miles (1km) from the gate, where the road forks, take a left along a concrete path past vegetable allotments.

❺ Keep following signs to Tung Chung, passing Loh Hon Temple.

FARTHER AFIELD WALK

101

Excursions

FARTHER AFIELD EXCURSIONS

THE BASICS

Distance: 75 miles (120km)

Journey Time: 45 minutes (high-speed train) or 20 minutes (plane)

🚄 Express from Western Kowloon Terminus, 34 trains run daily 8.05am–10.50pm: 12 trains run daily 7.25am–8.01pm

✈ From Chek Lap Kok

ℹ Yitai Square, Guangzhou

GUANGZHOU

The capital of Guangdong province is both the crucible of Cantonese culture and China's historic economic powerhouse. Alongside Beijing and Shanghai, it's been at the forefront of China's modern transformation and the dynamism is palpable. Culture vultures will also find temples and the best restaurants in China.

Guangzhou makes for an interesting one- or two-day trip from Hong Kong. Its history can be traced back to the third century BC when the area was settled by the armies of the first emperor, Qin Shi Huangdi. By the end of the first millennium AD, the city was an international port and it became one of the chief trading places as China opened up to overseas merchants from the 16th century.

Shamian Island is Guangzhou's most charming locale. Originally a sandbar on the Pearl River, the island was reclaimed and divided into foreign concessions after the Opium Wars of the mid-19th century. North of Shamian is the Qingping Market. Many stalls have moved inside in beautification and hygiene campaigns. Nevertheless, the area is charming for its old-world ambience and architecture.

In the east of the city is a gridded district with hotel towers, offices, the avant-garde Zaha Hadid-designed Guangzhou Opera House and the excellent Guangdong Museum. Across the river is one of the tallest structures in China, the 1,969ft (600m) Canton Tower. There's a tourist observation deck and a stomach-churning ride on the tower's spire. For an eclectic range of shops and cafés, explore the Tianhe North district where spots like HAY Coffee and So Acai punctuate the traditional residential areas.

MACAU

Many people come to Macau for the cobbled streets, baroque architecture and cuisine of Portugal's last colony (surrendered in 1999). More still come to gamble at the world's biggest casino capital.

Macau is compact and most of the main places of interest can be seen in a day or two. Highlights include the ruined facade of 17th-century St. Paul's Cathedral and the Jesuit Monte Fortress. Hotels and good restaurants are easy to find, and prices are notably lower than those in Hong Kong. The things to buy here are antiques, jewelry and gadgets. Rua de São Paulo has lots of antiques shops, as well as stores selling Asian handicrafts. Lago de Senado has clothing shops and local restaurants. To see a different Macau, make your way to Taipa or Coloane—villages that seem locked in time with low-rise architecture, cafés and cobbled streets.

THE BASICS

Distance: 37 miles (60km)

Journey Time: 1 hour by jetfoil 🚢 Jetfoil from the Shun Tak Centre, Connaught Road or China Ferry Terminal, Canton Road 💰 Expensive ℹ️ Largo do Senado, Edificio Ritz No. 9, Macau ☎ 8397 1120. Hong Kong: Shop 336, Shun Tak Centre, Connaught Road ☎ 2857 2287 ❓ Carry passport; no visa needed for North Americans or Europeans for 30–90 days, depending on the country

SHENZHEN

Shenzhen is where China's first capitalist experiments kicked off in the 1980s. It is China's richest metropolis. Culture is at a premium but there are also massive theme parks.

Among them, you'll find Splendid China, a theme park where the Great Wall, the Forbidden City and the Terra-cotta Warriors, among other monuments of Chinese art and architecture, are reduced to one-fifteenth of their real size. The China Folk Culture Village introduces the country's ethnic minorities.

But the real draw here is the excellent shopping, and you'll find that prices are lower than in Hong Kong. At Luohu Commercial City, connected to the train station, you can spend a day shopping for homeware, bags, watches, gadgets—or get a suit or dress tailored in less than a day.

THE BASICS

Distance: 25 miles (40km)

Journey Time: 40 min 🚇 MTR from Tsim Sha Tsui East to border at Lo Wu and Lok Ma Chau ❓ Visas for US visitors must be obtained in advance at travel agents in Hong Kong. Visa regulations change so check before you finalize your plans. Single-entry 5-day visas are issued at the border for some Western passport holders (**NB: not available to US citizens**).

Shopping

A PORTA DA ARTE

Tucked down a narrow alley on Macau's main peninsula, A Porta Da Arte sits inside a 60-year-old building that once served as a factory. Today, it is a lovingly renovated four-story space which is a hub for creative industries. There's a cosy Triangle Coffee Roaster café on the ground floor, an indie lifestyle store filled with local designs, a jewelry-making workshop, a make-up artist's studio, as well as a pretty rooftop that's teeming with greenery.

➕ Off map ✉ 42 Rua dos Ervanários, Macau ☎ 853 6345 6588 ⏰ Daily 11–8 🚇 No MTR

CITYGATE OUTLETS

citygateoutlets.com.hk

Located at the end of the Tung Chung line, Citygate Outlets is the city's largest outlet mall and the best place to shop for discounted luxury products—think fashion, sporting goods, beauty, home decor, accessories and more. There are more than 80 international upscale brands with prices marked down by 30 to 70 percent, depending on the season. While you're there, stop in to one of the 16 restaurants or catch the nearby Ngong Ping Cable Car to see the Big Buddha up close.

➕ Off map ✉ 20 Tat Tung Road, Lantau Island ☎ 2109 2933 ⏰ Daily 10–1 🚇 Tung Chung

DONGMEN PEDESTRIAN STREET

A satisfying blend of old and new, popular Dongmen Pedestrian Street is one of the most buzzing areas of Shenzhen. In this commercial epicenter, shops swell with everything from cultural handicrafts to clothes, while clusters of traditional Chinese-styled malls stock accessories, knock-offs and food courts. With a little bit of patience and a knack for bargaining, you'll find some treasures.

➕ Off map ✉ Dongmen Middle Road, Shenzhen 🚇 Laojie

LO WU COMMERCIAL CITY

Right beyond the Chinese customs you'll step inside this vast complex of shops selling, well, everything. Anything you saw and liked in Hong Kong, including last year's designer outfits at low, low prices, is probably here. It's particularly good if you are considering some quick tailoring, want to buy some textiles to take home, or you're in the market for some designer copies. Take care of your personal property and bring toilet paper with you.

➕ Off map ✉ Lo Wu 🚇 Lo Wu KCR ❓ Visas issued at border for many Western passport holders (NB: not US citizens)

NGONG PING VILLAGE

np360.com.hk

This village has been created as part of the Ngong Ping 360 tourism project and is designed to engender a sense of the original culture of this area. Next to the cable car terminal, it's an ideal spot to pick up souvenirs.

➕ Off map ✉ Lantau Island 🚇 Tung Chung, then Skyrail

THE SHOPPES

venetianmacau.com

Macau's Sands Shoppes, at The Venetian Hotel, is a shopper's delight built around a "canal." It's the place to go if you're looking for high-end designer goods.

➕ Off map ✉ Macau 🚢 Jetfoil from Shun Tak Centre, Connaught Road or China Ferry Terminal, Canton Road ❓ Take your passport (▷ 103, Macau Basics panel)

Where to Eat

360° BAR, RESTAURANT & LOUNGE ($$$)

The views are top-notch, to say nothing of the wine list and decor at this chic venue, which focuses on premium imported steaks. It's just a short stroll from the Hong Kong border in Shenzhen, inside the Shangri-La Hotel.
➕ Off map ✉ Shangri-La Hotel, 1002 Jianshe Lu, Luohu, Shenzhen ☎ 755 8396 1380 ⏰ Daily 6–11pm 🚇 Shenzhen

THE 8 RESTAURANT ($$$)

grandlisboahotels.com/en/grandlisboa/dining/the-8

Awarded three Michelin stars for the past six years, The 8 Restaurant is the pinnacle of Chinese fine-dining in Macau. Book well in advance to dine at this esteemed address, where you'll discover more than 40 types of delicate dim sum and over 16,900 wine labels.
➕ Off map ✉ 2/F, Grand Lisboa, Avenida de Lisboa, Macau ☎ 853 8803 7788 ⏰ Mon–Sat 11.30–2.30, 6.30–10.30, Sun 10–3, 6.30–10.30 🚢 Macau Ferry

ALBERGUE 1601 ($$$)

albergue1601.com

Nestled in St. Lazarus Quarter, a beautiful heritage district in central Macau, Albergue 1601 pays homage to the city's Portuguese history with its flavors and ambience. Don't leave without trying Head Chef Pedro Almeid's addictive piri piri chicken, baked duck rice and suckling pig.
➕ Off map ✉ 8 Calçada da Igreja de São Lázaro, Macau ☎ 853 2836 1601 ⏰ Daily noon–3, 6–10.30 🚢 Macau Ferry

A LORCHA ($$)

alorcha.com

Meaning "wooden ship" in Portuguese, A Lorcha celebrates the fusion of Chinese and Portuguese cuisine with quintessential dishes such as dried cod cakes, seafood soup, African chicken, Portuguese sausage, and lots of sangria. A lively atmosphere and friendly staff add to the experience.
➕ Off map ✉ 289 Av. Almirante Sergio, Macau ☎ 853 2831 3193 ⏰ Wed–Mon 12.30–3, 6.30–11 🚢 Macau Ferry

BATHERS RESTAURANT ($$$)

bathers.com.hk

Bathers Restaurant is worth the trek to Lantau Island's Cheung Sha Village. The beautifully designed alfresco space provides front-row seats to the ocean and delicious Mediterranean food.
➕ Off map ✉ 32 Lower Cheung Sha Beach, Lantau ☎ 2504 4788 ⏰ Tue–Fri noon–10, Sat–Sun 9am–10pm 🚢 Lantau

CHINA BEAR ($$)

chinabear.com.hk

Known for its feel-good vibes, China Bear is a great spot to kick back and relax. The pub-style restaurant is right by the waterfront by the Mui Wo ferry pier.
➕ Off map ✉ G/F, Mui Wo Centre, Mui Wo, 3 Ngan Wan Road, Lantau Island ☎ 2984 9720 ⏰ Mon–Fri 11–3, Sat 8.30–3, Sun 8.30am–midnight 🚢 Lantau Ferry

DYNASTY 8 ($$)

sandscotaicentral.com/restaurants/chinese/dynasty-8.html

Taking diners on a culinary journey, Dynasty 8 channels the opulence of the

ancient Chinese dynasties with creative dim sum creations, carefully prepared seafood, and specialty soups. A vegan menu is also available.

🔲 Off map ✉ 1/F, Conrad Macao, Sands Cotai Central, Macau ☎ 853 8113 8920 🕐 Mon–Fri 11–3, Sat–Sun 10–3, 6–11 🚢 Macau Ferry

GOA NIGHTS ($$$)

goanights.com

Inspired by Goa, a former Portuguese enclave on India's western coast, this bohemian restaurant specializes in contemporary tapas, curries and sharing plates. The cocktail menu's equally enticing, peppered with signature drinks inspired by the voyages of Vasco de Gama.

🔲 Off map ✉ 118 R. Correia da Silva, Macau ☎ 853 2856 7819 🕐 Tue–Thu 6pm–1am, Fri 6pm–midnight, Sat–Sun noon–4, 6pm–midnight 🚢 Macau Ferry

HAIDILAO ($$$)

haidilao.com

Haidilao isn't your typical Sichuan hot pot joint. Instead of a frills-free experience, this upscale address delivers serene interiors, attentive staff and high-quality dishes ordered via an iPad. Try a four-compartment pot if you'd like to sample multiple broths.

🔲 Off map ✉ 5-6/F, Youyicheng, 63 Youyi Road, Luohu District, Shenzhen ☎ 755 8225 0991 🕐 Daily 24 hours 🚇 Shenzhen

ROBUCHON AU DOME ($$$)

grandlisboahotels.com/en/grandlisboa/dining/robuchon-au-dome

Begun by the late, great Joel Robuchon, the Robuchon au Dome has a glitzy location atop the Grand Lisboa Hotel and has earned three Michelin stars. Given that this is one of Asia's top

eateries, the lunches are a particularly good value. But if you're coming here to celebrate a special occassion, we'd recommend going all out for the set dinner menus with perfectly chosen wine pairings.

🔲 Off map ✉ 43rd Floor, Grand Lisboa Hotel, Avenida do Infante D. Henrique, Macau ☎ 853 8803 7878 🕐 Daily 12–2.30, 6.30–10.30 🚢 Macau Ferry

SHANG PALACE ($$$)

shangri-la.com/shenzhen/shangrila/dining/restaurants/shang-palace

An upscale Cantonese dining experience, Shang Palace at the Shangri-La Hotel Shenzhen prepares classic recipes with only the most premium ingredients. Signature dishes include crispy pork flambé with Chinese rose wine and traditional double-boiled chicken soup.

🔲 Off map ✉ 2/F, Shangri-La Hotel Shenzhen, 1002 Jianshe Road, Shenzhen ☎ 755 8396 1383 🕐 Mon–Fri 11–3, 5.30–10.30, Sat–Sun 9–4, 5.30–10.30 🚇 Shenzhen

---

DINING 101

Don't want to look like a tourist at Hong Kong's local restaurants? Follow these simple pointers:

In some local restaurants there might be a bowl of hot water in the center of each table. Use this water to wash all of your eating utensils before digging in.

At most restaurants, you'll find two pairs of chopsticks at your place setting: One pair to use when plucking food from the sharing plates, and one pair for eating. After eating, place your chopsticks on the provided rest.

NB: Never cross them or stick them vertically into your rice—both gestures are associated with death and funerals.

Half the fun of your stay in Hong Kong is finding and enjoying your hotel, whether it be five-star luxury or more basic accommodations, where you can meet other guests and exchange travelers' tales.

Introduction

The Hong Kong hotel scene is divided between cheap rooms for budget-seeking travelers, and options for wealthy Chinese and the globetrotting foreign elite whose tariffs range from the very expensive to the eye-watering. Those looking for middle-of-the-road rooms in familiar branded hotels will find the city surprisingly expensive, but, if one is more adventurous, there are bargains to be had. Serious luxury is concentrated on either side of Victoria Harbour while, as a rule, hotels become cheaper the farther north in Kowloon or the New Territories you are prepared to go.

Budget Hotels

Space is at a premium in Hong Kong, so most rooms are likely to be smaller than you expect, even luxury accommodations. The really budget places tend to be guesthouses in Tsim Sha Tsui, in some of the very old apartment blocks. Be prepared for cramped rooms, little security and few facilities, but you get to stay right at the heart of the action for very little outlay. Walk around Tsim Sha Tsui with your backpack and the guesthouses will find you.

Online Reservations

Making reservations online can save you money, with some excellent last-minute deals to be found. Fall (autumn) through to Chinese New Year (usually January or February) sees reservations at their peak, and any major trade fairs in Hong Kong and Guangzhou also cause prices to spike. However, the heat of summer brings lower prices and good deals.

HOTEL TIPS

Check breakfast rates before you make a reservation. Most hotels offer a bed-and-breakfast promotion and the better ones could fill you up for the day. Places that offer late breakfast (say until 11am) are worth seeking out, especially if you are a night owl. If you are staying in a budget place, bring your own padlock. Some places offer lockers to store your things.

Budget Hotels

PRICES
Expect to pay between HK$300 and HK$700 per night for a budget hotel.

BISHOP LEI INTERNATIONAL HOUSE

bishopleihtl.com.hk

Toward the upper end of the budget spectrum, Bishop Lei is a friendly, business-like hotel and is in a great Mid-Levels location. A choice of standard and double rooms cost HK$700.

➕ C10 ✉ 4 Robinson Road, Mid Levels, Central ☎ 2868 0828 🚇 Central then Mid-Levels Escalator

CARITAS BIANCHI LODGE

caritas-chs.org.hk

Tidy, clean and well-run, Caritas is a go-to for affordable accommodations. The amenities are limited to laundry and the restaurant.

➕ F5 ✉ 4 Cliff Road, Yau Ma Tei ☎ 2388 1111 🚇 Yau Ma Tei

HONG KONG HOSTEL

hostel.hk

If you're looking for the best value for budget accommodations on the island, this hostel provides a series of rooms in a block of apartments, most with a private bathroom, phone, fridge and TV.

➕ H10 ✉ Flat A2, 3rd Floor, Paterson Building, 47 Paterson Street, Causeway Bay ☎ 2392 6868 🚇 Causeway Bay

MOJO NOMAD ABERDEEN HARBOUR

mojonomad.com

For a hotel-meets-hostel experience, try Mojo Nomad Aberdeen Harbour down on the southside of Hong Kong Island. This beautifully designed hotel is home to a trendy bar, co-working areas and a choice of shared or private accommodations. A bed in a shared dorm here goes for about HK$400.

➕ Off map B12 ✉ 100 Shek Pai Wan Road, Aberdeen ☎ 3728 1000 🚇 Aberdeen

NEW GUANGZHOU GUESTHOUSE

This relatively high-quality guesthouse in Chungking Mansions feels slightly removed from backpacker conditions. It's very simple, and rooms are small, but the air-conditioned, en-suite singles go for HK$150 and it's only a minute from the MTR station.

➕ F7 ✉ Flat D6, 13/F, Block D, Chungking Mansions, 36-44 Nathan Road, Tsim Sha Tsui ☎ 2311 2005 🚇 Tsim Sha Tsui

SPIN HOTEL

Located right by the Ladies' Market and the Nathan Road shopping district, Spin Hotel offers nine basic rooms—all with WiFi, air conditioning, housekeeping and private bathrooms. You can book a standard room for an extremely reasonable HK$400.

➕ F3 ✉ 2/F Wing Wah Building, 22–22A Sai Yeung Choi Street South, Kowloon ☎ 2311 2005 🚇 Tsim Sha Tsui

CHUNGKING MANSIONS

A massive residential and commercial complex in Tsim Sha Tsui, Chungking Mansions has long been the first port of call for backpackers visiting Hong Kong. It's still the cheapest place to stay in Hong Kong, but the disadvantages of the cramped, inadequate elevators and heavily populated staircases outweigh the financial savings. Instead of sleeping here, we'd recommend visiting Chungking Mansions for its excellent Indian, African and Pakistani restaurants which are all hidden on the upper tower floors.

Mid-Range Hotels

PRICES

Expect to pay between HK$700 and HK$2,000 per night for a mid-range hotel.

ACESITE KNUTSFORD HOTEL

acesitehotel.com

Sitting right atop buzzing Knutsford Terrace, a premier nightlife hub in TSim Sha Tsui, Acesite Hotel is convenient, affordable and comfortable. The rooms include basic amenities, such as air conditioning, ironing boards, TV, private bathroom and more. Single rooms can be booked from HK$1,000.

➕ F7 ✉ 8 Observatory Court, Tsim Sha Tsui, Kowloon ☎ 2377 1180 Ⓜ Tsim Sha Tsui

EATON HONG KONG

eaton-hotel.com

Eaton Hong Kong offers a range of stylish rooms, as well as restaurants, a swimming pool, gym and a food hall. Catch any bus stopping outside the door to get to Tsim Sha Tsui. There's also a co-working space on site, should you need to squeeze in some work.

➕ F6 ✉ 380 Nathan Road, Yau Ma Tei ☎ 2782 1818 Ⓜ Jordan

GLOUCESTER LUK KWOK

gloucesterlukkwok.com.hk

This is a good value, centrally located, business-oriented hotel. The rooms are small and all on the floors above the 19th. You'll also find restaurants and a residents' cocktail bar.

➕ F10 ✉ 72 Gloucester Road, Wan Chai ☎ 2866 2166 Ⓜ Wan Chai

HOTEL COZI OASIS

hotelcozi.com/oasis

A bit out of the way in Kwai Chung industrial district, about 25 minutes northwest of Central by MTR, Hotel Cozi Oasis offers 583 well-priced rooms. Expect contemporary design plus amenities including WiFi and a complimentary smartphone to borrow during your stay. There's a restaurant, bar and gym. Rooms from HK$900.

➕ Off map ✉ 43 Castle Peak Road, Kwai Fung ☎ 3891 1888 Ⓜ Kwai Hing Station

HOTEL PANORAMA

hotelpanorama.com.hk

A high-rise in the thick of Tsim Sha Tsui, Hotel Panorama sports a contemporary design with lots of dark wood and mirrors. There are wide harbor views, interrupted only by a couple of tower blocks. The top-floor restaurant and bar are outstanding.

➕ F7 ✉ 8A Hart Avenue, Tsim Sha Tsui ☎ 3550 0388 Ⓜ Tsim Sha Tsui

HOTEL STAGE

hotelstage.com

A gem of a hotel in the old-school Yau Ma Tei district, Hotel Stage is artsy yet approachable. The rooms are among the best value in the area, with modern design, powerful showers and comfy beds. While you're there, make time to try the in-house restaurant and bar. Doubles from HK$1,500.

➕ F7 ✉ 1 Chi Wo Street, Yau Ma Tei ☎ 3550 0388 Ⓜ Tsim Sha Tsui

KOWLOON HOTEL

harbour-plaza.com/kowloon/Index-en.htm

This is a modern place with many facilities but tiny rooms. However, each room has free WiFi, while some have harbor views. Breakfast is not included in rate, but you can tack it on for a reasonable price.

➕ F8 ✉ 19–21 Nathan Road, Tsim Sha Tsui ☎ 2929 2888 Ⓜ Tsim Sha Tsui

LAN KWAI FONG HOTEL @ KAU U FONG

lankwaifonghotel.com.hk

Promising a great location and excellent value, this boutique hotel features oriental decor and lots of facilities, including a gym and WiFi. The suites are a bit more expensive but have extensive views over the city. The homey atmosphere and ideal location give it an advantage over some of the 5-star hotels.

🔢 C9 ✉ 3 Kau U Fong, Central ☎ 3650 0000 🚇 Central

THE LUXE MANOR

theluxemanor.com

A boutique hotel with chic, avant-garde interiors near Knutsford Terrace, The Luxe Manor feels larger than life. From the giant wooden swing doors of the lobby, to the scarlet bins in the rooms, it oozes glamor. This one is for bohemians and fashionistas.

🔢 F7 ✉ 39 Kimberley Road, Tsim Sha Tsui ☎ 3763 8888 🚇 Tsim Sha Tsui

THE MIRA HOTEL

themirahotel.com

This chic and boutiquey hotel has a good spa and a choice of restaurants. The Mira is also in a great location, right opposite Kowloon Park.

🔢 F7 ✉ 118 Nathan Road, Tsim Sha Tsui ☎ 2368 1111 🚇 Tsim Sha Tsui

NATHAN HOTEL

nathanhotel.com

You can expect big rooms in this small and quiet place close to Jordan MTR. It's well run, with everything you need to get by, including an in-room smart phone to use.

🔢 F6 ✉ 378 Nathan Road, Tsim Sha Tsui ☎ 2388 5141 🚇 Jordan

ROSEDALE

rosedalehotels.com.hk

Rosedale is a conveniently located hotel in Causeway Bay, close to the shops. All the usual facilities in the room plus a small gym, WiFi and business services.

🔢 H10 ✉ 8 Shelter Street, Causeway Bay ☎ 2127 8888 🚇 Causeway Bay

ROYAL PARK HOTEL

royalpark.com.hk

The Royal Park Hotel has large rooms and excellent facilities, including a pool and a free shuttle bus into town. If you don't mind the half-hour ride each day, this is a great value. It's close also to excellent walks and parks in the New Territories.

🔢 Off map ✉ 8 Pak Hok Ting Street, Sha Tin ☎ 2601 2111 🚇 Sha Tin MTR

ROYAL PLAZA HOTEL

royalplaza.com.hk

Located a little bit out of the center in Mong Kok, this hotel is close to some great bargain shops and markets. The hotel's connected to the Mong Kok East train station and MOKO shopping center, so it's easy to get around the city. There's also a good Chinese restaurant, an all-day buffet in the Western restaurant, a gym, sauna and outdoor swimming pool.

🔢 F3 ✉ 193 Prince Edward Road West, Mong Kok ☎ 2928 8822 🚇 Mong Kok MTR

STANFORD HILLVIEW

stanfordhotels.com.hk/hillview

The Stanford Hillview is a small, quiet hotel near the Knutsford Terrace nightspot. It offers an all-day buffet room, WiFi and free smartphone service. There is a shuttle service to the airport train.

🔢 F7 ✉ 13–17 Observatory Road, Tsim Sha Tsui ☎ 2722 7822 🚇 Tsim Sha Tsui

Luxury Hotels

PRICES
Expect to pay more than HK$2,000 per night for a luxury hotel.

CORDIS, HONG KONG

cordishotels.com/en/hong-kong

The only 5-star hotel in Mong Kok, Cordis, Hong Kong has an impressive line-up of guest facilities with huge rooms and enormous marble tile bathrooms, great service and, best of all, a really good spa complete with private treatment rooms and all kinds of health and beauty treatments.

➕ E4 ✉ 555 Shanghai Street, Mong Kok
☎ 3552 3388 🚇 Mong Kok

THE FOUR SEASONS

fourseasons.com/hongkong

Beautifully designed with loving attention to detail, the Four Seasons offers guests the utmost in comfort. Bars, restaurants, and a stunning rooftop swimming pool with underwater music.

➕ C9 ✉ 8 Finance Street ☎ 3196 8888
🚇 Central

INTERCONTINENTAL HONG KONG

hongkong-ic.intercontinental.com

This elegant hotel, with good *feng shui*, has some of the best views of the island across the harbor. Great swimming pool. Award-winning Cantonese restaurant and Rech by Alain Ducasse are among the top dining options.

➕ F8 ✉ 18 Salisbury Road, Tsim Sha Tsui
☎ 2721 1211 🚇 Tsim Sha Tsui

ISLAND SHANGRI-LA

shangri-la.com

Towering above Central with amazing views over the city, this luxurious hotel has spacious, well-designed rooms, some great places to eat and drink and the world's longest Chinese painting. Good fitness suite and pool. Library for guests.

➕ E11 ✉ Pacific Place, Supreme Court Road, Central ☎ 2877 3838 🚇 Central

MANDARIN ORIENTAL

mandarinoriental.com/hongkong

The very central Mandarin Oriental has a long tradition of impeccable service. Well-appointed rooms, with attention to detail, helpful staff, classy shops, great pool, excellent restaurants. It has reopened after a huge refit and is looking better than ever.

➕ D10 ✉ 5 Connaught Road, Central
☎ 2522 0111 🚇 Central

RITZ-CARLTON HONG KONG

ritzcarlton.com/hongkong

A sumptuous hotel lodged in the uppermost floors of one of Hong Kong's tallest buildings. There are two Michelin Star-winning restaurants, the world's highest bar (▷ 72) and a spectacular spa-with-a-view. Rooms have 42-inch TVs as standard, and imposing marble bathrooms. A splurge option.

➕ D6 ✉ 103rd–118th Floor, International Commerce Centre, 1 Austin Road West, Kowloon ☎ 2263 2263 🚇 Kowloon

ISLAND OR KOWLOON?
If you want to stay at one of the top-drawer hotels in Hong Kong you need to decide whether you want to stay on the island or in Kowloon. Some of the hotel chains, such as Shangri-La, have hotels in both areas and most of them have amazing views across the harbor. If you love to stay in your room, then Kowloon has better views of the nightly Symphony of Lights, but if you're a nightlife lover then the island is the place for you.

This section offers all you need to know about Hong Kong, from how to pay your tram fare to where to go to find WiFi, to opening hours and health precautions—all the ins and outs of a visit.

Planning Ahead

When to Go

The ideal time to visit is between October and mid-December, when the days are warm and fresh and the nights are cool. Try to avoid June through September, when the weather is extremely hot and humid. The hotels are at their most expensive from late fall to early February.

TIME

Hong Kong is 8 hours ahead of the UK, 12 hours ahead of New York and 15 hours ahead of Los Angeles.

AVERAGE DAILY MAXIMUM TEMPERATURES

JAN	FEB	MAR	APR	MAY	JUN	JUL	AUG	SEP	OCT	NOV	DEC
64°F	63°F	66°F	75°F	82°F	84°F	88°F	88°F	84°F	81°F	73°F	68°F
18°C	17°C	19°C	24°C	28°C	29°C	31°C	31°C	29°C	27°C	23°C	20°C

Spring (March through May) is usually warm, although rain is common.
Summer (June through September) is very hot and humid, with nearly 16in (400mm) of rain on average each month. The clammy heat sometimes gives way to violent typhoons.
Fall (October through to mid-December) is usually warm.
Winter (mid-December through February) is comfortable, with occasional cold spells.
Typhoons hit between July and September. Hotels post the appropriate storm signal: Storm Signal 1=Typhoon within 500 miles (800km) of Hong Kong; Storm Signal 3=Typhoon on its way, be prepared; Storm Signal 8=Stay in your hotel, dangerous winds with gusts.

WHAT'S ON

January/February *Chinese (Lunar) New Year*: This holiday looms large in Hong Kong life. The harbor fireworks display is magnificent, but the crowds are enormous.
Mid-February/mid-March *Arts Festival*: International orchestral, dance and theater events over four weeks.
March *Hong Kong Sevens*: This rugby tournament is a wild three-day-long party.
Late March/April *International Film Festival*: Lasts for two weeks; various venues.

April *Ching Ming*: Tomb-sweeping day.
Tin Hau Festival: Tin Hau temples remember a 12th-century legend about a girl who saves her brother from drowning. Fishing junks and temples are decorated and Chinese street operas held near the temples.
Birthday of Lord Buddha (late April to early May): At temples Buddha's statue is ceremonially bathed, symbolically washing away sins and material encumbrances.
May/June *Dragon Boat Festival*: Noisy, dragon-boat

races are held to commemorate the political protests of a 4th-century poet and patriot, Chu Yuan.
August/September *Hungry Ghosts Festival*: Offerings of food are set out to placate roaming spirits in this traditional Buddhist festival.
September/October *Mid-Autumn Festival*: Families head out with lanterns and eat mooncakes to commemorate the fullest moon of the year.

Hong Kong Online

discoverhongkong.com
The official website of the Hong Kong Tourism Board. Information about Hong Kong, suggestions for days out, history, transportation, etc.

timeout.com.hk
Lots of information on what's on, restaurant reviews and shopping tips, all aimed at a young audience.

new.gayhk.com
Intel about Hong Kong's gay scene, places to visit, reviews of clubs, bars and more.

scmp.com
This is the site of the *South China Morning Post,* the territory's major newspaper. News items, cultural information, current affairs.

thestandard.com.hk
Breaking news from Hong Kong's second English-language newspaper.

littleadventuresinhongkong.com
This stellar tour company provides in-depth walking tours with a focus on food.

grayline.com.hk
A well-established tour company offering tours of the island and trips into China.

hongkongairport.com
The site of Hong Kong International Airport provides useful information before you arrive.

hkclubbing.com
This site keeps track of the new and not-so-new clubs, as well as latest events in the city.

sassy.com
Aimed at women and families, Sassy provides up-to-date information about shopping, dining, pampering and events.

USEFUL WEBSITES

fodors.com
A comprehensive travel-planning site. You can research prices and weather, reserve air tickets, cars and rooms, ask questions (and get answers) from fellow visitors, and find links to other sites.

mtr.com.hk
Information on the metro system in Hong Kong. Details of Octopus cards, airport express, tourist passes and many other useful details.

tripadvisor.com
Website selling hotel deals, which has reviews by visitors, many of them very candid.

WIFI ACCESS

Almost every café or restaurant in Hong Kong has WiFi these days, but you often need to ask for a password and, at the very least, buy a drink in order to log on. In addition, the MTR has free WiFi at every station.

Getting There

ENTRY REQUIREMENTS

All visitors must hold a valid passport. For the latest passport and visa information, look at website immd.gov.hk.

VISITORS WITH DISABILITIES

Generally speaking wheelchair users will find that the newer buildings have good access while older buildings and most streets, MTR stations, footbridges (of which there are hundreds) and shopping centers are difficult to navigate. Taxis, ferries and some buses are wheelchair friendly.

The Hong Kong Council of Social Services
🏢 11th–13th Floor, Duke of Windsor Social Services Building, 15 Hennessy Road, Wan Chai ☎ 2864 2929, hkcss.org.hk

AIRPORTS

All flights land at Hong Kong International Airport at Chek Lap Kok, 15 miles (24km) west of Hong Kong city.
The two terminals of the airport include three banks, a moneychanger, several ATMs, a tourist information office and acres of restaurants and bars.

18 miles (30km)
12 miles (20km)
6 miles (10km)
✈ **Chek Lap Kok Airport**   ● **Hong Kong**

ARRIVING AT HONG KONG INTERNATIONAL AIRPORT

For airport information call 2181 0000 or visit hongkongairport.com.

The Airport Express (tel 2881 8888; mtr.com.hk) is the most efficient way of getting to town from the airport. Trains depart for the city at 12-minute intervals from 5.50am to 12.48am; journey time to Central is 24 minutes, to Kowloon 18 minutes; cost HK$115 one way to/from Central, HK$100 to/from Kowloon, returns costing HK$305/HK$185 respectively.

If you use the Airport Express on your return journey you can check in your luggage at Hong Kong or Kowloon stations. Some airlines allow check-in at these stations one day in advance.

There are also bus services into Hong Kong Island, Kowloon, the New Territories and Lantau Island, which are less expensive. Information can be obtained from the tourist office in the airport or citybus.com.hk. The Citybus A11 travels into Hong Kong Island for HK$40, while the A21 serves Kowloon for HK$33.

A taxi to Hong Kong Island will cost around HK$350 and includes the toll fare for the Lantau Link. The journey to Kowloon costs around HK$270.

ARRIVING BY BUS

Bus services from Shenzhen and a host of Pearl River Delta (Guangdong) cities are provided by CTS Express coaches (tel 3604 0118). There are buses to downtown stops as well as direct buses from Shenzhen to the airport. To travel into China you must get a visa in advance of your journey.

ARRIVING BY TRAIN

The Guangzhou–Shenzhen–Hong Kong High Speed Railway opened in 2018, reducing the journey from Guangzhou to Hong Kong to about 45 minutes. The train departs from the Guangzhou South train station 34 times a day, arriving in Hong Kong's West Kowloon terminus. It's advised to buy train tickets online in advance, as this is a popular link for commuters. It's also advised to arrive 45 minutes before your train departs to allow time for immigration and customs. There are also rail links with Shanghai and Beijing. For booking and more information, visit the MTR's high-speed rail website: ticketing.highspeed.mtr.com.hk.

Slower trains travel from Guangzhou East railway station to Hung Hom 12 times a day, 8.19am–9.32pm.

EMBASSIES AND CONSULATES

- Australia: 23rd and 24th Floors, Harbour Centre, 25 Harbour Road, Wan Chai, tel 2827 8881.
- Canada: 12th–14th floors, Tower 3 One Exchange Square, 8 Connaught Place, Central, tel 3719 4700.
- Germany: 21st floor, United Centre, 95 Queensway, Central, tel 2105 8788.
- Portugal: 25th Floor, Yardley Commercial Building, 3 Connaught Road West, Sheung Wan, tel 2587 7182.
- Spain: Suite 5303, Central Plaza, 18 Harbour Road, Wan Chai, tel 2525 3041.
- UK: 1 Supreme Court Road, Admiralty, tel 2901 3000.
- US: 26 Garden Road, Central, tel 2523 9011.

INSURANCE

It is vital to have cover for medical expenses and accidents, as well as theft, baggage loss and trip cancellation. Check your insurance coverage and buy a supplementary policy as needed.

DEPARTURE TAX

Anyone over 12 years old pays HK$120 (in Hong Kong dollars only). This is included in the price of your airline ticket.

CUSTOMS REGULATIONS

- Duty-free allowance is 1 liter of spirits and (import) 19 cigarettes.

Getting Around

NGONG PING 360

Ngong Ping 360 is an aerial cable car linking Tung Chung with Ngong Ping on Lantau Island.

TRAINS

● The MTR (Mass Transit Railway) is the quickest way to hop between shopping areas on Hong Kong Island, Kowloon and the New Territories.

● Stations have clear instructions in both English and Chinese for operating ticket machines. Machines issue thin plastic tickets that are also available from information/ticket counters. Fares are between HK$25.5 and HK$55. Tickets have a magnetic strip and payment is made by tapping or, sometimes, as you insert your ticket into the machine as you pass through the ticket barrier.

● MTR maps are available at the airport and can be found in most hotel lobbies. MTR stations dispense a free guide to the system in English and Chinese. In addition, a mobile App is available for trip planning and fare calculation.

BUSES

Traveling on buses is not really recommended (except for trips to the south side of Hong Kong Island), but in the event of using one, note the fixed fare is marked on the bus as you enter and pay; no change is given. Tourist Board offices have a free map showing bus fares and routes.

TAXIS

Taxis are good value and can be picked up easily, although many drivers do not speak fluent English. Once inside you must use the seat belt.
● The flagfare for red "downtown" taxis is HK$24, and after a 1.5-mile (2km) distance the fare increases by HK$1.70 for every 210 yards (200m). There is an additional charge of HK$6 made for each large piece of baggage. Fares might be slightly different in the New Territories and Lantau.
● A "For Hire" sign is displayed in the wind-screen; a "Taxi" sign is lit up on the roof.
● Taxis are not supposed to stop at bus stops or on a double-yellow line.

TRAMS

● Trams run only on Hong Kong's north side—the route between Kennedy Town (west) and Causeway Bay (east) is one of the most useful.

● Destinations are marked on the front in English.

● The fixed fare of HK$2.30 is dropped in the paybox before leaving the tram or payable by Octopus Card.

THE OCTOPUS CARD

If you are planning to stay in Hong Kong for any length of time, consider buying an Octopus Card (HK$150). This is a prepaid card that can be used on most of the city's transport systems, as well as in shops, restaurants and other businesses to replace cash. The card is not personalized in any way and the HK$50 deposit required is refundable. However, the card operates in the same way as cash so if lost or misplaced the cash value is also lost. You can check the balance of cash remaining on the ticket each time you use it.

ORGANIZED SIGHTSEEING

● Splendid organizes personalized tours of Hong Kong and South China, including an Aberdeen or harbor night cruise, horse racing (June–September), Lantau Island and a Splendid Night of Delight, as well as tours into China (tel 2316 2151; splendidtours.com).

● Water Tours Ltd. conducts six different harbor cruises, including a sunset junk cruise on Victoria Harbour (tel 2926 3868; watertours. com.hk).

● Star Ferry runs 19 harbor tours a day (tel 2118 6201; starferry.com.hk).

● Grayline Tours offers city tours, dinner cruises and day trips to China (tel 2368 7111; grayline.com.hk).

● Little Adventures Hong Kong specializes in Hong Kong's culinary history. These walking tours are a must for foodies and anyone who's curious to learn more about Cantonese cuisine (littleadventuresinhongkong.com).

EMERGENCY NUMBERS

Police/Fire/Ambulance
☎ 999

THE MID LEVELS

Special to Hong Kong is the 15-minute trip up to the Mid Levels on escalators. The series of escalators begins in Central, on Des Voeux Road, and extends up through the many residential tiers in hilly Central.

NEED TO KNOW GETTING AROUND

Essential Facts

OPENING HOURS

● Offices: Mon–Fri 9–5, Sat 9–1.
● Banks: Mon–Fri 9–5, Sat 9–12.30.
● Post offices: Mon–Fri 9.30–5, Sat 9.30–1.
● Shops: Daily 10–6, often 10–9/11–11 in tourist areas.

MONEY

The unit of currency is the Hong Kong dollar (= 100 cents). Notes come in denominations of 10, 20, 50, 100, 500 and 1,000; coins are 10, 20 and 50 cents, and 1, 2, 5, 10 dollars.

LOST PROPERTY ON MTR

✉ Admiralty MTR station; Tai Wai, Siu Hong Kong station
🕐 Daily 8–8
☎ 2861 0020

ETIQUETTE

● Shaking hands is common practice, as is the exchanging of business cards, presented with both hands.
● Don't be surprised when people push, shove and jump the line or fail to line up at all.
● A service charge is usually added to restaurant bills. Round up taxi fares to the next five to 10 dollars.

MEDICAL TREATMENT

● Outpatient departments of public or private hospitals provide emergency treatment.
● Private doctors (see Yellow Pages) charge HK$150 per visit on average. This usually includes three days' medication.
● Public hospitals:
Queen Mary Hospital (102 Pok Fu Lam Road, Hong Kong Island, tel 2855 3838)
Queen Elizabeth Hospital (30 Gascoigne Road, Kowloon, tel 2958 8888).
Kwong Wah Hospital (25 Waterloo Road, Yau Ma Tei, Kowloon, tel 2332 2311).
● Private hospitals:
Adventist (40 Stubbs Road, Wan Chai, Hong Kong Island, tel 2574 6211).
Baptist (222 Waterloo Road, Kowloon Tong, tel 2339 8888).

MONEY MATTERS

● Traveler's checks can often be cashed at banks or moneychangers. Always check the exchange rate before making any transaction; banks offer the best rates. There are scores of small streetside moneychangers (particularly in Tsim Sha Tsui and Causeway Bay). It's safe to change cash here, though shop around for the best deal as rates vary.
● Credit cards—Visa, MasterCard, American Express and Union Pay are widely accepted for purchases in shops and restaurants, and can be used to obtain cash from banks as well as ATM machines.
● Most Hong Kong Bank teller machines provide 24-hour HK$ withdrawal facilities for

Visa and MasterCard holders. Amex holders have the same facility at some Jetco ATMs, as well as the Express ATMs.

NATIONAL HOLIDAYS

Dates of the Chinese lunar festivals vary from year to year.
● 1 January: New Year's Day.
● Late January or early February: Chinese New Year (three days).
● March/April: Good Friday and Easter Monday.
● Early April: Ching Ming Festival.
● 4 April/early May: Buddha's birthday.
● 1 May: Labor Day.
● Mid- to late June: Dragon Boat Festival.
● 1 July: Hong Kong SAR Establishment Day.
● Late September or early October: Mid-Autumn Festival.
● 1 October: China National Day.
● Mid- to late October: Cheung Yeung Festival.
● 25 and 26 December: Christmas Day and Boxing Day.

NEWSPAPERS, MAGAZINES, TV AND RADIO

● International newspapers and magazines are available in bookstores, newsagents and hotel kiosks. The newsagent at the Star Ferry terminal in Tsim Sha Tsui has a good selection.
● There are two English-language daily newspapers: the broadsheet *South China Morning Post* and the tabloid *Hong Kong Standard*.
● For entertainment listings look for *Time Out Hong Kong*.
● The two main TV stations, TVB and viuTV, each has one channel broadcast mainly in English—TVB Pearl and Channel 96—though Mandarin and Cantonese are interspersed.
● Public radio broadcaster RTHK has only one English-language channel, but does provide a live feed of the UK's BBC World Service.
● Web-based media outlets such as *Sassy*, *Foodie*, *ButterBoom* and *Zolimba City Magazine* are popular for local lifestyle content.
● For family and wellness news, try *Hong Kong Living*, *Hong Kong Moms* and *Liv* magazine.

SENSIBLE PRECAUTIONS

● Keep wallets and purses secure.
● Keep traveler's checks separate from the invoice that lists their numbers.
● Don't leave valuables where you can't see them at all times.
● Keep travel documents and money in a hotel safe.
● Hong Kong is similar to, and often safer than, European or North American cities.
● Public transportation at night is as safe as during the day.

ELECTRICITY

● The current is 200/220 volts, 50 cycles alternating current (AC).
● Most wall outlets take three square-pronged electricity plugs.
● US appliances require a converter and a plug adaptor.

POST OFFICES

The General Post Office on Hong Kong Island is at 2 Connaught Place, Central.
● In Kowloon, the main post office is at the ground floor of the Kowloon Government Offices, 405 Nathan Road, Yau Ma Tei.
● Letters and postcards to destinations outside Southeast Asia cost up to HK$5 for weight up to 20g.
● The Speedpost service cuts the usual five-day service to Europe or North America by about half. Go online to speedpost.hongkongpost.hk.

STUDENT TRAVELERS

● There are few discounts for ISIC (International Student Identity Card) holders.
● Some places of interest have a reduced student admission price.

TELEPHONES

● Local calls are free from private homes. Public phones charge HK$1 per call and sometimes only take HK$2 coins without giving change. Pressing the "FC" (follow-on call) button before hanging up allows a second call.
● Phonecards, available in denominations of HK$50 and HK$100 at 7–Eleven stores and other shops, are easier to use, especially for International Direct Dialling calls.
● For IDD calls, dial 001, followed by the country code and then the area code (minus any initial 0) and number. Dial 013 for information about international calls.
● To call Hong Kong from abroad dial 00 852, then the 8-digit number.

TOILETS

● Most are Western style.
● Hotels or shopping malls are the best places to find clean toilets.
● Most coffee shops will let you use their toilet if you purchase a drink first.
● Public toilets are free.
● If you plan to use a public toilet, be sure to take toilet paper with you.

Language

Hong Kong has two official languages: Cantonese and English. While English is spoken widely in business circles and tourist areas, it is not always understood elsewhere. It's best to get the hotel receptionist to write down your destination in Chinese. A few words of Cantonese will go a long way in establishing rapport —and off-the-beaten track they may prove very useful.

BASICS	
neih wuih mwuih gong ying mahn?	Can you speak English?
jóu sahn	Good morning
néih hou ma?	How are you?
wai! (pronounced 'why')	Hello (only on the phone)
mgòi	Thank you (for a favor)
dò jeh	Thank you (for a gift)
mgòi	Please
mgòi	Excuse me
deui mjyuh	I'm sorry
haih or hou	yes
mhaih or mhou	no
bin douh?	where?
fèi gèi chèung	airport
bā si	bus
dihn chè	tram
géi dō?	How many/how much?
géi dō chin?	How much is it?
géi dim jung?	What time is it?

NUMBERS	
leng	
yāt	0
yih	1
sàam	2
sei	3
ngh	4
luhk	5
chát	6
baat	7
gáu	8
sahp	9
sahp yāt	10
yih sahp	11
yih sahp yāt	20
saam sahp	21
sei sahp	30
ngh sahp	40
luhk sahp	50
chát sahp	60
baat sahp	70
gáu sahp	80
gáu sahp gáu	90
yāt baak	99
yāt chihn	100
	1000

Timeline

WORLD WAR II

In 1937, hundreds of thousands of Chinese, displaced by the Japanese invasion of China, sought refuge in Hong Kong. On December 8, 1941, Japanese aircraft bombed Kowloon, and by Christmas Day the British had surrendered. More than 2,000 people died and 10,000 soldiers were taken prisoner. British civilians were incarcerated in Stanley Prison. With the surrender of the Japanese in August 1945, Hong Kong again became a British colony.

4000BC Early settlement left some pottery, stone tools and iron implements—then for many centuries the islands had more pirates than farmers.

C200BC The Chinese Empire is unified and for the next millennium-and-a-half Hong Kong Island is ruled by a governor based in Canton.

1685 British and French merchants begin to deal in tea and silk. The British later start to import opium as a way of extending their power and profits.

1839–42 Chinese attempts to block the import of opium end in defeat; the treaty concluding the first Opium War cedes Hong Kong Island to the British "in perpetuity." Within two decades, another treaty concedes the Kowloon Peninsula. In 1889 a further treaty leases substantial land north of Kowloon—the New Territories—to Britain for 99 years.

1941–45 Japanese occupation (▷ panel, this page).

1949 The Communist victory in China leads to refugee influxes.

Murray House, a former government building; an old post box; Lei Cheng Uk Museum; a flag-raising ceremony; Golden Bauhina next to Hong Kong Convention Centre (left to right)

1950–53 When the US imposes sanctions against China during the Korean War the colony develops a manufacturing base of its own.

1967 The political passions rocking China spill over into Hong Kong, with riots and strikes. The colony seems on the brink of a premature closure of its lease, but normality soon returns.

1975 100,000 Vietnamese refugees arrive.

1982 British Prime Minister Margaret Thatcher goes to Beijing to discuss the colony's future.

1984 The Sino-British Joint Declaration confirms the return of the colony to China. In 1988 Beijing publishes its Basic Law for Hong Kong citizens, guaranteeing their rights.

1989 The Tiananmen Square massacre confirms Hong Kong's fears about its future under China's sovereignty. A million people protest on the streets of Hong Kong.

1997 Hong Kong becomes a Special Administrative Region of China. English remains an official language. People from other parts of China require special approval for entry.

2003 SARS epidemic hits Hong Kong.

2017 The 20th anniversary of the Handover of sovereignty from Britain to China.

2018 The Hong Kong–Zhuhai–Macau Bridge officially opens as the longest over-sea bridge in the world.

THE HANDOVER

At midnight on June 30, 1997, Britain's last vestige of empire was handed back to the Chinese. Trepidation surrounded the occasion, but in the event it was a muted affair in one of the worst rainstorms in memory. Few people were on the streets. Chris Patten, Hong Kong's last governor, and Prince Charles quietly and tearfully slipped away on the royal yacht *Britannia* and the Red Army silently drove across the border. The expatriate workers who had not chosen to leave marked the occasion in Lan Kwai Fong bars, and everyone woke up the next day a little nervously, wondering how their lives would be changed, and a little shocked that nothing seemed different.

Index

Hong Kong 25 Best

WRITTEN BY Joseph Levy Sheehan and Graham Bond
UPDATED BY Kate Springer
SERIES EDITOR Clare Ashton
COVER DESIGN Jessica Gonzalez
DESIGN WORK Liz Baldin
COLOR REPROGRAPHICS Ian Little

Published in the United Kingdom by AA Publishing.

ISBN 978-1-6409-7201-8

EIGHTH EDITION

Printed and bound in China by 1010 Printing Group Limited

10 9 8 7 6 5 4 3 2 1

A05671
Maps in this title produced from mapping © MAIRDUMONT / Falk Verlag 2013 and data available from openstreetmap.org © under the Open Database License found at opendatacommons.org
Transport map © Communicarta Ltd, UK

We would like to thank the following photographers, companies and picture libraries for their assistance in the preparation of this book.

All images are copyright AA/B Bachman, except:

2-18 The Peak Hong Kong; 6c AA/N Hicks; 6br AA Photodisc; 7tcr Courtesy of Hong Kong Tourism Board; 7tr Courtesy of Hong Kong Tourism Board; 7cl Courtesy of Hong Kong Tourism Board; 10tcr Goods of Desire; 11tcl AA/N Hicks; 13(iii) Aqua; 16tr AA/A Mockford & N Bonetti; 16/7b Courtesy of Hong Kong Tourism Board; 17tl Courtesy of Hong Kong Tourism Board; 17tcl AA/D Henley; 17cb Courtesy of Hong Kong Tourism Board; 18tr Courtesy of Leisure and Cultural Services Department of Hong Kong; 18tcr AA Stockbyte; 18cr Courtesy of Ocean Park Hong Kong; 20 Courtesy of Hong Kong Tourism Board; 26 Jason Knott / Alamy Stock Photo; 27 Zoonar GmbH/Alamy Stock Photo; 28tl Hong Kong Park; 28tr AA/A Kouprianoff; 29l AA/A Kouprianoff; 29r AA/N Hicks; 30tl AA/N Hicks; 31tl Courtesy of Ocean Park Hong Kong; 31tc Courtesy of Ocean Park Hong Kong; 31tr Courtesy of Ocean Park Hong Kong; 34–35 Tai Kwun; 36l AA/D Henley; 36/37 AA/D Henley; 37tr AA/D Henley; 37crb AA/D Henley; 37c AA/D Henley; 38/9 The Peak Hong Kong; 38/9t The Peak Hong Kong; 39cr The Peak Hong Kong; 41-42t AA/N Hicks; 42bl Hong Kong Zoological and Botanical Gardens; 46t Sevva; 47t Sevva; 48t Courtesy of Hong Kong Tourism Board; 49t Courtesy of Hong Kong Tourism Board; 50t Courtesy of Hong Kong Tourism Board; 51 Photo is provided by the Leisure and Cultural Services Department, the Government of Hong Kong Special Administrative Region; 54tl AA/N Hicks; 56tl AA/N Hicks; 56tc AA/D Henley; 56tr AA/A Kouprianoff; 60cl AA/N Hicks; 61 AA/D Henley; 62/63 Symphony of Lights; 66 Photo is provided by the Leisure and Cultural Services Department, the Government of Hong Kong Special Administrative Region; 67-69t Courtesy of Hong Kong Tourism Board; 67b AA/D Henley; 68bl Courtesy of Hong Kong Tourism Board; 68br Sky 100 Hong Kong Observation Deck; 72t Sevva; 73t Sevva; 74t Courtesy of Hong Kong Tourism Board; 75t Courtesy of Hong Kong Tourism Board; 76t Courtesy of Hong Kong Tourism Board; 80t Hong Kong Wetland Park of the Agriculture, Fisheries and Conservation Department; 80cl Courtesy of Hong Kong Wetland Park; 80cr Hong Kong Wetland Park of the Agriculture, Fisheries and Conservation Department; 81 Hong Kong Wetland Park of the Agriculture, Fisheries and Conservation Department; 84tl AA/A Kouprianoff; 84tr AA/A Kouprianoff; 85bl Courtesy of Hong Kong Tourism Board; 86b AA/A Kouprianoff; 88 Kau Sai Chau Golf Course; 89c Sevva; 90t Courtesy of Hong Kong Tourism Board; 94/95c Courtesy of Hong Kong Tourism Board; 96l Courtesy of Hong Kong Tourism Board; 97t Courtesy of Hong Kong Tourism Board; 98b Courtesy of Hong Kong Tourism Board; 99b © Steve Vidler/Alamy; 100 Jason Knott/Alamy Stock Photo; 101t 102t AA/I Moprejohn; 102bl AA/I Moprejohn; 102bc AA/A Kouprianoff; 102br AA; 103t AA/D Henley; 103bl AA/D Henley; 105t Courtesy of Hong Kong Tourism Board; 106t Courtesy of Hong Kong Tourism Board 108-112t AA/C Sawyer; 108tcr The Ritz Carlton, Hong Kong; 108cr The Luxe Manor; 108br The Ritz Carlton Hong Kong; 124bl Courtesy of Hong Kong Tourism Board; 125bc Courtesy of Hong Kong Tourism Board; 125br AA/D Henley

Every effort has been made to trace the copyright holders, and we apologize in advance for any accidental errors. We would be happy to apply the corrections in the following edition of this publication.

Titl~~es in the~~

MAP INCLUDED